BOLD PIES THAT WILL CHANGE
YOUR LIFE . . . AND DINNER

REVOLUTIONARY
PIZZA

DIMITRI SYRKIN-NIKOLAU
FOUNDER OF **DIMO'S PIZZA,** HOME OF CHICAGO'S
MOST DISTINCTIVE PIES

PAGE STREET
PUBLISHING CO.

PAGE STREET
PUBLISHING CO.

First published in 2014 by
Page Street Publishing Co.
27 Congress Street, Suite 103
Salem, MA 01970
www.pagestreetpublishing.com

Distributed by Macmillan; sales in Canada by The Canadian Manda Group; distribution in Canada by
The Jaguar Book Group.

17   16   15   14   1   2   3   4   5

ISBN-13: 978-1-62414-050-1
ISBN-10: 1-62414-050-5

Library of Congress Control Number: 2013955155

Cover and book design by Page Street Publishing Co.
Photography by Ted Axelrod

Printed and bound in China

Page Street is proud to be a member of 1% for the Planet. Members donate one percent of their
sales to one or more of the over 1,500 environmental and sustainability charities across the
globe who participate in this program.

THIS BOOK IS DEDICATED TO ALL THOSE
WHO HAVE SLAVED AWAY IN A KITCHEN
PREPARING FOOD, SELFLESSLY AND
WITHOUT PRAISE, SO THAT
OTHERS MAY ENJOY IT.

IN THE CRUST
WE TRUST.

DIMOSPIZZA.COM
773 525 4580

DIMOSPIZZA.COM
773 525 4580

DIMOSPIZZA.COM
773 525 4580

DIMOSPIZZA.COM
773 525 4580

DIMOSPIZZA.COM
773 525 4580

DIMOSPIZZA.COM
773 525 4580

DIMOSPIZZA.COM
773 525 4580

THIS
WAY
TO AN
ALTERNATE
PIZZA

CONTENTS

TAKE ANOTHER LITTLE PIZZA MY HEART

FOREWORD

I have never won a Pulitzer, nor the National Book Award, not even the booby prize for "Best Book About Pro Wrestling and Pot." But it no longer matters because I have been humbled with the greatest literary accolade of them all—Dimo's Pizza named a pizza after me in honor of one of my books. In the hierarchy of great literary huzzahs, there ain't nothin' better. The problem, of course, is that I now have little left to live for.

I am from New York and know a few things about pizza. And beginning with my first primitive salvos as a teenaged miscreant, I have personally innovated over 14,000 variations of the toaster oven pizza bagel. But I cannot touch the ingenuity and painterly imagination of Dimitri, the colossal superbrain behind this book and Dimo's Pizza. He is like the Jasper Johns of pizza chefs. Or, if you prefer, the Willy Wonka.

Dimitri's vision of pizza knows no limits: from his sweet pies (Celia's Sweet Peach Cobbler!) to any of his deconstructed dinner pies, because pizza really is a blank canvas upon which to write our dreams in mashed potatoes and gravy.

Did I mention they named a pizza after me? The greatest day of my life! Not even if the Carnegie Deli suddenly got hip and started offering a sandwich of sardines and red onions on pumpernickel rye as "The Edison" could I possibly be prouder. That the last guy who had a pizza named for him was former WWE Champion CM Punk made it that much sweeter. He sold attitude. The guys who had sammies named after them at the Carnegie sold neuroses.

I was on the road promoting my book *Dirty! Dirty! Dirty!*—a history of sex on the newsstand—when I got the call from Dimitri telling me that the Dimo's brain trust had "convened" (a powwow that boggles the imagination) and decided that they were going to bestow the honorific totem of a proprietary pizza on me and my book just as soon as I got to Chicago, and that the Dirty Pie would most likely involve sausage of some kind.

Pizza is the food of the people and Dimitri is their Spartacus. Pizza knows no class or race or social status. It is enjoyed by all the citizens of the earth, from presidents and kings to lowly stoners, metalheads, hip-hoppers, punk rockers, Michelin-starred restaurateurs, rule-breaking professional wrestlers and perennially award-winning authors. But who needs literary kudos from a bunch of eggheads when you can have a pizza with your name on it?

In the end, the Mike Edison Dirty Pie evolved from a simple sausage fest to an orgy of Roman proportions, if the Romans had lived in New Orleans. It was a fully realized gumbo pizza with okra, shrimp and andouille sausage, and I am not kidding when I say that seeing my name attached to such genius and putting the thing in my mouth was the greatest thrill of my life—what I imagine being the first man on the moon must have been like.

Screw the Pulitzer. Gimme gimme some pizza! God bless Dimo's! Gabba gabba hey!

Mike Edison
New York City

Writer and musician Mike Edison is the former publisher of *High Times* magazine. His books include *I Have Fun Everywhere I Go: Savage Tales of Pot, Porn, Punk Rock, Pro Wrestling, Talking Apes, Evil Bosses, Dirty Blues, American Heroes, and the Most Notorious Magazines in the World* and *Dirty! Dirty! Dirty!: Of Playboys, Pigs, and Penthouse Paupers—An American Tale of Sex and Wonder*.

INTRODUCTION

Welcome to an alternate pizzaverse!

We'd rather you not call this a cookbook. To be honest, these recipes are far from complex in the realm of culinary knowledge or cooking techniques. Instead of recipes, consider these pages inspiration for your next party, ammunition to shock your in-laws at the annual holiday gathering, and really good excuses to keep the utensils and plates in the cabinet.

If we're really honest, this is more of a look into how we approach our craft. Our mantra: pizza is the food of the people. It's accessible. It's cheap. And most of all, it's comforting. We see pizza crust as our canvas for creating and re-creating our favorite meals in new and unthinkable ways. And maybe we're gluttons for groupies, but we love the satisfaction of causing a memorable reaction.

Selling pizzas with French fries and macaroni noodles on the regular, we've learned that pizza is kind of a big deal. Over the years, we've come to define a few specific reactions that remind us why we do what we do.

The first is the "Silent Admiration." We know we've found a new "crustomer" for life when we spot this reaction. It's all in the facial expressions. When the silent, glossy-eyed admirer gazes into the syrup-drizzled face of Chicken n' Waffles pizza, there's no denying the bond that's just been formed.

The second we'll affectionately call "Earmuffs." It's interesting how pizza with bacon and ranch can somehow bring out the beast in people. All in a flash, we not only just heard words we certainly hadn't planned to hear uttered in public, but these words (we'd classify them as N-17 rated adult words) were also in fact describing the very pizza we just made.

The third is the "Oh-No-You-Didn't" reaction. We always do our best to make every crustomer happy and informed about what they are eating. But in the case of the "Oh-No-You-Didn't" it seems that with each ingredient we list off, the crustomer gets equally more upset and enticed. This reaction is accompanied by an abundance of knee-slapping, gasping, clapping and usually ends with a, "Can I hug the cook?"

So what's the point here? Making ridiculously crazy pizza is both delicious and entertaining when shared with others. You never know what reactions you'll get when you turn, say, a Reuben sandwich into a pizza (in that case, it was very close to a teary-eyed gasp from a large bearded man).

Onto a slightly less pizza and slightly more business note:

We wouldn't feel right making this book and not sharing a little bit about our business philosophy with you though in truth, that's probably another book in and of itself. If this is your first time meeting us, (nice to meet you!) we're a pizza-by-the-slice restaurant from the Windy City with offbeat and unconventional flavors. We're sure you've probably already surmised that much from the title of the book, but you may not have known that we're also in the field of building unconventional or nontraditional business practices.

Who exactly is the "we" that we're talking about? Well obviously there isn't a collective group of Dimo's employees sharing a keyboard to write this book. But much like the social nature of pizza, our company functions in many ways through collaboration. In each of our employees, we scout out brainstormers and adventure seekers with a passion for learning and a desire to take a stake in our business.

In fact, many of the recipes in this book can be accredited to our employees in one way or another. They've done everything from generating new ideas and testing pizzas, to selling, promoting and gathering feedback from our crustomers. That's because we believe a job at Dimo's should provide more than just a place to clock in and out; it's a place to develop skills and pursue passions. And truthfully, pizza can only be as relevant, innovative and radical as the people who help create it.

Crafting new pizza concepts is a job that will never tire us. There will always be a new idea to develop, an old recipe to make better and a new person to work with. That's where you come in. When we were offered the opportunity to make a cookbook, we knew it had to be more than just slapping some of our favorite recipes together. This was our chance to share our approach and pizza philosophy with a much bigger audience.

We hope that once you've cooked your way through some of these recipes you'll start to understand what it takes to make a great pizza. Then, the real magic can happen. You can start to build your own recipes, alter and tweak the pizzas provided here to suit your tastes and become the master of your own pizzaverse. That's our true goal. And please, don't forget to spread the word and share a slice or two with those around you. One last thing! Remember: unless otherwise noted, each recipe yields one 12 inch/30.5 cm pizza.

So, without further ado, welcome to the team! You're now officially ready to roll up your sleeves and start the dough tossing.

1

THE BASICS: MAKING 'ZA MAGIC

Please be advised: if you're a novice in the craft of pizza making, this chapter will be your new best friend. You can't make a proper 'za without the right ratio of dough, sauce and toppings. In the following pages, we'll attempt to re-create our own recipe for this magic ratio—including how to make your own hand-tossed dough. That's right: you're about to become one part ace baker, one part master chef and one part artistic virtuoso.

We'll go ahead and tell you right now, it's not going to be easy. But we've always believed that perseverance in the kitchen yields delicious payoffs. It's like all forms of art: the more you practice, the more you refine, the better you'll do. Give yourself a few chances. When you make dough, go ahead and make a double batch so you have extra to work with. Hell, make a triple batch if you need to. Just don't stop until you get it right. You got this! And on top of the personal accomplishment you'll feel, you'll likely become pretty popular when you share your handiwork. What you need to know is that you should read through the entirety of this section before beginning. Yeah, we know you probably won't. But if you do, we promise it'll turn out better!

THE DOUGH

No matter how crazy the toppings, a winning pizza always starts with quality dough. In our kitchen that means dough that becomes a light, crisp, foldable crust. It has just a hint of sweetness, with versatility to pair with our inventory of offbeat flavors. It's also important for our recipe that you use high-gluten flour and cold water. The high-gluten flour will ensure the proper texture and the cold water will help control the dough's rising process. But all of the recipes in this book will work with just about any type of dough, keeping in mind that cook times will vary from what we have. This recipe makes about two 12 inch/30.5 cm dough balls.

- -

1 cup and 1 tbsp/252 mL of cold water

2 tsp/10 g salt

2 tbsp/25 g sugar

1 tbsp/15 mL extra virgin olive oil

2 tsp/6 g dry yeast or 1 tsp active wet baker's yeast

3½ cups/420 g high-gluten flour

Cornmeal and flour for rolling the dough

In a mixer combine water, salt, sugar and oil. Whisk together by hand. Add in yeast and quickly whisk, then immediately add the flour. Mix at medium speed using a dough hook for about 10 minutes until dough ball forms.

The best consistency for fully mixed dough is such that it's sticky, but not so sticky that it will leave residue on everything it touches. If the dough is a little on the sticky side, sprinkle a little flour on top of the dough and mix it manually with your hands. Cut the dough into two equal-sized balls.

Knead the dough with your hands about ten times over to get out any air bubbles in order to create a smooth surface after kneading. Knead the dough with the purpose of forming it into the shape of a ball. A dough ball is ready for proofing when its surface is completely smooth, like a marble. Place the dough onto a smooth surface (a plate is ideal) and cover it with a moist towel.

Once you've fashioned the dough balls, let them sit out for a minimum of two hours. The hotter the ambient temperature, the less time the dough will need to rise. The colder, the more time it will need. You know you're ready to go when the dough balls have risen to about twice their original size.

If you're ready to make pizza now, go for it! Otherwise, place the dough in the refrigerator to slow the rising process until you're ready to assemble your pizza. Making dough and getting it to rise can be a process, so be sure to check out *A Few More Doughy Tips* on the next page for details on a more in-depth explanation on the science behind making perfect dough.

IT'S ALIVE! HANDLING YEAST

We prefer to use wet baker's yeast, but sometimes that can be tricky to find at your local grocery store. You may want to contact your favorite local bakery to see if they've got a little extra you can use. But if you can only find dry yeast, make sure that what you're using isn't expired. You want the yeast to be active and to do its job—you're counting on it!

Another note about yeast: it's important for the wet yeast not to come in direct contact with salt because this will kill the yeast and prevent it from rising. That is why you whisk ingredients together before adding the yeast, so the two ingredients don't come into direct contact.

A FEW MORE DOUGHY TIPS

Getting dough to the right size is all about balancing water temperature, yeast quantities and air temperature. It's the metabolism of sugar by yeast: converting carbohydrates to carbon dioxide and alcohol. The carbon dioxide output that takes place inside the dough is what makes the dough rise in size. Like many reactions, this process can be controlled by the addition and subtraction of ingredients and the regulation of temperature.

Cooler temperatures (below 55°F/13°C) will slow the rising process. Bringing the dough out to warmer temperatures will speed up the rising process. Once the dough gets above 55°F/13°C, the yeast will become most active and start the reaction.

To bring out the best flavor, you want your dough to proof for at least 24 hours in the fridge. So it's best to make your dough the day before you plan to assemble and bake your pizza. It won't be bad if you use it right after two hours as we suggested earlier, but it'll be better if you let it hang out in your fridge overnight. You'll know that the dough is ready to use when you press it in with your fingers and it slowly springs back to retain its shape.

The other tangible benefit of letting the dough sit in your fridge for some time is that you get to control the timing. So you've got a party tomorrow? No problem! Just make a few batches of dough today, let it rise and then put it in your fridge until you're ready.

FROM DOUGH BALL TO PIZZA (LET'S GET STRETCHING!)

Pizza party tip: it's always easier to stretch dough that's warm. If the dough is in the fridge, take it out about 20 minutes before you're ready to stretch it.

Remember, it can take a great deal of practice to become proficient at stretching dough by hand. It's an arduous art form. If you don't succeed at first, try again. I know it seems like we've said that a lot and that's because it's warranted. Most of all, don't take it too seriously. This is just pizza, people. It's meant to be fun!

OKAY, IT'S GO TIME

1. Coat the entirety of the dough in a 50/50 ratio of ground cornmeal to flour mixture. Place the dough on a nonporous surface that you'll stretch the dough on. Marble, granite or laminate work well. Place the dough in the same orientation that it was sitting when rising, with the surface that was exposed to the air during rising faceup. Press down with your fingertips, forming a depressed circle in the center of the dough.

2. Adding extra cornmeal and flour mixture to your work surface should make it significantly easier for you to stretch the dough. It will stop the dough from sticking.

3. Flip the dough over so that the side that wasn't exposed to air during the rising process is faceup. Place the outside of your pinky (of your nondominant hand) and the outside of your hand on the crust about two fingers width from the edge.

4. Rotate the dough in a circular manner and use the outside of your hand like a plow tilling the land to create a crust on the outer edge of the dough about the width of just one finger. If your left hand is dominant, rotate the dough counterclockwise. If your right hand is dominant, rotate clockwise. The goal is to end up with a ring of crust that is even in size.

5. Push down on the dough in the middle with the tips of your fingers to push out any extra bubbles. Don't be afraid to use force!

6. Flip the dough over. Place your fingers just inside the crust and pull them away from each other in small motions. The point of contact on the dough should be the pads of your fingers and the force should be distributed evenly. After you pull your hands apart, rotate the dough. Continue until you've made one full rotation. This act should stretch the outer 3 inches/8 cm of dough, but do nothing to the middle of the dough.

NEXT COMES TOSSING THE DOUGH

At this point, you should have a clearly defined crust around the edge of the pizza but the interior of the pizza should be of identical thickness throughout.

The shape of your hands and the position of your hands on the dough are the two most important things when it comes to tossing the dough. If you're looking at your left hand, form the letter C. The letter begins at the tip of your index finger and curves around to end at the top of your thumb. Your middle, ring and pinky fingers should be in uniform shape directly behind the index finger with no spaces between them. Mimic this shape on your right hand and you've got the shape of your hands covered.

1. Place the dough on top of your knuckles and keep your two hands about 3 inches/8 cm apart.

2. Gently pull your hands apart and then toss the dough into the air so as to rotate it. Before doing this, choose what direction you want to rotate the dough. Some people find counterclockwise easier, others clockwise. Go with whatever feels most natural.

3. Continue to pull your hands apart while rotating the dough in a circular manner so that each time the dough gets tossed into the air it falls back on your knuckles. Your knuckles should be touching a portion of the dough that is slightly to the left or right of where your knuckles just were. Basically, you're inching your way around the outer edge of the dough, expanding the diameter of the pizza with each toss.

4. Continue to do this until the dough is about 12–14 inches/30–37 cm in diameter. The number of times you'll need to toss the dough in the air is a function of the temperature and consistency of your dough and your level of experience. Lower temperature dough and inexperience will make it take longer for you to stretch the dough.

OH NO, A HOLE!

If you tear the dough, don't worry. It can be repaired. Put it down on your working surface and pull the dough over the tear. Press down hard to reconnect the dough. Add a pinch of flour to keep that spot from sticking later. Voila! You're good to go!

THE SAUCE

Here are some of our go-to sauces. You'll use these recipes for many of our pizzas in this book. You can also use these to create your own new pizza flavors! They make great foundations for new pies.

- -

ALFREDO SAUCE

- -

4 CUPS/950 ML

3 tsp/15 g butter
¼ cup/25 g flour
1 qt/1 L heavy cream
2 tsp/10 g salt
2 tsp/5 g ground black pepper
½ cup/90 g Parmesan
1 tbsp/10 g fresh garlic, minced

Start by mixing the butter and flour in a large pan on medium heat until the butter melts. Then add all other ingredients. Stir on medium heat for 10 minutes or until it boils. Place in the fridge for about 10 minutes to thicken before using.

SIMPLE CREAM

- -

4 CUPS/950 ML

1 cup/235 mL sour cream
2½ cups/590 mL heavy cream
1 egg
1 tsp pepper

Blend all ingredients together using a hand mixer or blender.

SPICY PESTO

----

1 ½ CUPS/355 ML

2 cups/80 g fresh basil leaves
¼ cup/30 g pecans
10 cloves garlic
1 tbsp/10 g red pepper flakes
1 tsp salt
1 tsp black pepper
¾ cup/177 mL olive oil
1½ tbsp/22 mL lemon juice

Roughly tear basil leaves. Combine basil, pecans, garlic, red pepper flakes and salt and pepper in food processor. Blend together and slowly drizzle in olive oil and lemon juice until fully combined.

CLASSIC MARINARA

----

3 CUPS/710 ML

1 cup/237 mL tomato paste
1 cup/160 g ground tomatoes
1 tbsp/3 g oregano flakes
1 tbsp/10 g granulated garlic
1 tbsp/10 g black pepper
1 tbsp/15 g sugar
1 cup/237 mL water

Combine all ingredients in a large mixing bowl. Use a hand mixer until the ingredients are well blended. Do not mix too fast or splashing will occur. This can be done by hand if necessary.

SAUCY TIPS AND TRICKS: It's best to sauce the pie on an appropriate prepping surface. A wooden pizza paddle or a wooden cutting board will work so that you can easily transfer the pizza to the preheated pizza stone. When you apply marinara, the best thing to use is a small ladle both to place the marinara on the pizza as well as to spread it across the pizza. For most pizzas, approximately 6 ounces/177 mL of sauce is appropriate.

When it comes to saucing a pie, there are three main ways we apply the sauce evenly to our dough.

1. Pour the sauce into a squeeze bottle and apply even rings to the dough, starting at the outside closest to the crust and working toward the center. If you don't have a squeeze bottle, we recommend using a spoon to gently drizzle the sauce over the pie. This option is messier and takes a steady hand to avoid uneven saucing.

2. For thicker sauces and gravies, we use a spatula to spoon out the sauce and very gently apply it evenly to the dough. For this type of saucing, you'll need to double-check that the dough isn't stuck to the working surface after you sauce the pie due to the pressure you've applied to it. Apply extra flour or cornmeal to your prep surface to help counteract this issue.

3. The last way is the most traditional saucing technique, which we only use for good ol' classic marinara pies. See below for detailed steps on this process.

MARINARA SAUCE HOW-TO

When you apply marinara, the best thing to use is a small ladle both to place the marinara on the pizza as well as to spread it across the pizza. For most pizzas, approximately 6 ounces/177 mL of sauce is appropriate.

1. Place the sauce directly in the middle of the pizza.

2. To spread the sauce, rotate the ladle in a spiral shape, starting from the middle and moving toward the edge, pushing the sauce outward with each rotation of the ladle.

3. Push the sauce right to the inner edge of the crust, but not over it.

4. Don't press too hard with the ladle to avoid leaving areas void of sauce.

5. Make sure you're pushing all the sauce away from the center to avoid a pool of sauce in the middle of the pie. Pools of sauce make for messy slices.

6. When you're done, you should have an even layer of sauce atop the pie and you shouldn't be able to see the white of the dough anywhere except for the crust at the edge of the pizza.

THE TOPPINGS

A delicious pizza requires the right balance of toppings to sauce and crust. As with any meal, you don't want one flavor to overpower the others. Remember that the crust we use is thin, and you won't want to add so many ingredients that you lose the flavor of your crust. Ultimately it's on you to judge the amount of toppings you think will make the best flavor palette.

Don't force on extra ingredients just because you have them. Instead, save them and create something just as delicious the next day. The ingredients can be turned into something else, but you can't remake the pizza once it goes into the oven. Remember, it's all about balance, kemosabe.

HERE ARE A FEW MORE TIPS FOR GETTING YOUR TOPPINGS JUST RIGHT

- Always place ingredients on a pizza from the outside in. It forms lines that you can color in.
- As with everything, the better quality mozzarella you use the better the pie you're going to get.
- Top a pie with the intention of getting a little bit of every flavor in every bite.
- The more ingredients you have, the less of each ingredient you'll need.

SPECIAL OF THE WEEK

great Gobble! Gobble!

VEGAN SPECIAL
ITALIAN

SUN DRIED TOMATOES, SPINACH
PENNE NOODLES, SAUSAGE SEITAN,
MOZZARELLA-TESE

(STALLION)

SLICES AND SALADS

THIS A WAY →

dimo's pizza

ORDER ONLINE DIMOS PIZZA.COM

DIMOSPIZZA.COM
773 525 4580

RESPECT YOUR MOTHER!

HOLY TRINIT

PIZZATIZERS

Whether you call them appetizers, hors d'oeuvres, finger foods or antipasto, the concept is the same: these culinary creations are made for partying. Essentially, if you're planning a celebration (see also: soiree, group hang, tailgate, etc) these pizzas should be invited. For that matter, please remember that no party is a real party unless it's a pizza party.

After all, 'za was created for socializing. Hey, if you enjoy shotgunning a whole pie by yourself, more power to you! But generally, you're not going to down an entire pizza solo in one sitting. With that in mind, we created an arsenal of pies that are not too heavy, not too difficult to prep and ready for sharing. And what better conversation starter than, "Wow, that's a Bloody Mary on a pizza? Totally rad!" Or, "O-M-G The Hulk is my favorite Avenger too! I can't believe you made him a pizza."

These are only a few examples of the raging pizza-themed parties in your future. So what are you waiting for? Commence 'za planning now.

SOUTHWEST EGG ROLL (UNROLLED)

Much like pizza, egg rolls take enticing ingredients and package them into an easily edible nugget of deliciousness. Those components are all still here, but this time in unrolled form. We'll go ahead and warn you now: this avocado sauce can be pretty addictive.

- -

ENOUGH DOUGH FOR 1 PIZZA (SEE P 19)

VEGETABLE MIX

3 tbsp/44 mL vegetable oil

½ cup/85 g red bell peppers, finely chopped

½ cup/50 g green onions, finely chopped

1 cup/220 g yellow corn

½ cup/15 g raw spinach, chopped

¼ cup/40 g jalapeños, finely chopped

1 tbsp/1 g fresh chopped cilantro

1 tsp cumin

½ tsp chili powder

½ tsp salt

½ tsp cayenne pepper

1 cup/260 g black beans, cooked

SAUCE

1 ripe avocado

½ cup/118 mL mayonnaise

½ cup/118 mL sour cream

2 tbsp/30 mL buttermilk

1 tbsp/15 mL white vinegar

¼ tsp salt

¼ tsp garlic powder

½ tsp ground black pepper

1 cup/113 g shredded pepper jack cheese

10 3" x 3"/ 8 x 8 cm wonton wrappers

3 cups/710 ml vegetable oil or enough to submerge the wonton strips for frying

For the vegetable mix, heat vegetable oil in pan and add red peppers and green onions. Cook until tender. Slowly stir in the corn, spinach, jalapeños, cilantro, cumin, chili powder, salt and cayenne pepper to the pan.

Cook for another 5 minutes. Add cooked black beans and heat for a few more minutes, stirring regularly. Once all ingredients are fully combined, let cool and set aside.

Cut the wonton wrappers into ½ inch x 3 inch/1 x 8 cm strips. Preheat saucepan with vegetable oil to 350°F/177°C. Fry strips until golden and crispy. Let cool on layered paper towels to help soak up excess oil.

For the sauce, blend all ingredients together in a food processor or blender until smooth.

Spread the vegetable mixture gently across dough in an even layer using a spatula. Bake in preheated oven for 10 minutes at 500°F/260°C until crust is golden brown. Remove from oven and add shredded pepper jack and crispy wontons to the hot pizza. Apply avocado sauce in rings, starting from the outside and working toward the center. Slice and serve.

THE GREAT CORNHOLIO

It's a pizza named for *Beavis and Butt-head*. What more could you really want from us? Extra points if you serve this pizza with your shirt over your head proclaiming, "I am the Great Cornholio!" Double extra points if you send us a picture of this. If nothing else, this will make for a memorable party favor. Recipe makes approximately two 12 inch/30.5 cm pizzas.

ENOUGH DOUGH FOR 2 PIZZAS (SEE P 19)

1 cup/170 g yellow cornmeal

1 cup/100 g flour

¼ tsp salt

¼ tsp baking soda

¼ cup/50 g sugar

3 tsp/11 g baking powder

1 egg

1 cup/237 mL buttermilk

1 package of all beef hot dogs (try tofu dogs for a veggie version)

All-purpose flour for coating the hot dogs

Vegetable oil (enough to submerge dogs for frying)

8 wooden skewers

Spicy mustard (amount up to your taste preference)

1¼ cup/113 g shredded mozzarella cheese

Mix cornmeal, flour, salt, baking soda, sugar and baking powder in large mixing bowl. Add egg and stir in milk until thoroughly combined.

Heat vegetable oil in pan until the temperature reaches approximately 350°F/177°C. Spear the dogs with skewers and roll them into extra flour. Then roll the floured dogs into the batter until evenly coated. Drop the battered dogs directly into the frying oil for approximately 3 minutes until light golden brown. Do not overcook or they will burn in the oven later.

Let the dogs cool completely. Remove skewers and cut dogs into ¼ inch/6 mm rounds.

If you're making two pizzas, remember to split the ingredients equally during this part. Apply most of the shredded mozzarella onto the doughs evenly. Distribute the corn dog pieces over the cheese. Add the rest of the mozzarella on top to keep pies from drying out in the oven. Bake for 10 minutes at 500 °F/260°C until crusts are golden. Remove from oven and apply rings of spicy mustard starting at the outsides moving toward the centers. Slice and serve.

YAYA'S SPANAKOPITA

You know this is authentic spanakopita because our Yaya said so. It works great for brunch or as a predinner appetizer to share with friends. Dill and feta cheese create a salty flavor, that'll make ya say, "Opa!'

ENOUGH DOUGH FOR 1 PIZZA (SEE P 19)

1 whole chopped yellow onion
Olive oil
2 cups/60 g spinach
1 cup/150 g Greek feta cheese
2 sprigs of fresh dill
1 egg
¾ cup/85 g shredded mozzarella
Fresh filo dough
Melted butter

Sauté the onion in olive oil. Add the spinach until blanched and condensed. Remove from heat and let cool. Squeeze out the water from this mixture with your hands. Add the feta cheese and mix together. Add the dill and the egg and mix.

Add the spinach, onion and egg mixture on top of the dough. Distribute shredded mozzarella over the mixture. Place a sheet of filo dough over the mixture and with a brush lightly spread melted butter onto each of the layers. Place a total of 4 sheets of filo dough on top of the pizza before baking in preheated oven at 500°F/260°C for 10–12 minutes until the crust is golden brown.

JALAPEÑO POP 'N' LOCK

Some pies are so tasty they lead to an obligatory happy dance. This is one of those pies. Actually, we know some people who would do just about anything to get a piece of this pie. One of our all-time most popular pizzas, it has a dance to go with it. Just how does one do the jalapeño pop 'n' lock? You'll have to make the pizza to find out.

- -

ENOUGH DOUGH FOR 1 PIZZA (SEE P 19)

BEER BATTER

⅓ cup/33 g all-purpose flour, plus extra for dipping

4 fl oz/118 mL of any pale lager (You can drink the rest of the can as you cook.)

1 egg

½ tbsp/8 g salt

⅓ cup/79 mL buttermilk

6–8 jalapeños, sliced to form rings (you may want to seed 'em too if you don't want it to be too spicy)

Salt and pepper

3–5 cups/710 mL–1L vegetable oil for frying (enough to submerge jalapeños in pan)

¼ cup/28 g shredded mozzarella

1 cup/237 mL cream cheese

½ cup/57 g shredded cheddar cheese

½ cup/140 g thick-cut bacon, fried and chopped

½ cup/25 g green onions, chopped

Mix ingredients for batter and submerge jalapeño slices in mixture. Set aside for 10 minutes.

Take extra flour and mix with a dash of salt and pepper. Preheat vegetable oil for frying to 375°F/190°C. Dip battered jalapeños into flour mixture and then into hot oil. Cook until browned. Using tongs, remove jalapeños and let extra oil drain. Set aside to cool.

Top the stretched dough with mozzarella cheese and bake for 5–7 minutes in preheated oven at 500°F/260°C. Remove the pizza, but leave the oven on. Apply the cream cheese using a baking spatula. Distribute fried jalapeño slices, then shredded cheddar evenly. Bake for 3–5 more minutes. Top with chopped bacon and green onions. Slice and serve... and dance.

SPINACH ARTICHOKE DIP

This slice was a happy accident: made on a whim one afternoon using ingredients we had on hand. It's still one of our most popular slices among our employees, despite never officially being added to our menu. Warning: this pizza is definitely made for garlic lovers. Vampires and hormonal teenagers beware (is there even a difference between those two groups anymore?). We recommend adding grilled or rotisserie chicken on top to make it a meal.

- -

ENOUGH DOUGH FOR 1 PIZZA (SEE P 19)

SAUTÉED SPINACH

4 cups/120 g raw spinach

2 tbsp/30 mL white zinfandel wine

1 tsp lemon juice

4¼ cups/1 L water

½ cup/118 mL olive oil

1 cup/150 g red onion, finely chopped

1 tsp fresh garlic, minced

1½ tbsp/23 g salt

16 oz/480 g of artichoke hearts

¾ cup/177 mL alfredo sauce (p 26)

3 tsp/10 g fresh garlic, minced

¾ cup/85 g shredded asiago cheese

Strain artichokes, removing all juice. Cut the artichokes loosely into small chunks and set aside.

Place spinach in a large mixing bowl. Pour wine and lemon juice over the spinach and set aside. In a large pot, add remaining ingredients for sautéed spinach. Bring to a boil over high heat. Pour hot water mixture into the large bowl over the spinach mix. Stir spinach until it wilts and condenses, then drain in a colander. Place drained spinach into refrigerator to chill.

Apply alfredo sauce in rings, starting from the outside of the crust and moving toward the center. Distribute spinach in small chunks, breaking apart pieces that stick together. Add artichokes. Sprinkle fresh garlic evenly over mixture. Bake for 10–12 minutes in preheated oven at 500°F/260°C until crust is golden brown. Add asiago immediately out of the oven. Slice and serve.

JAKE'S GRAPES

One thing is for certain: Jake's grapes make for some seriously sumptuous snackage. The bold flavors of blue cheese and pistachios are mellowed out with a light Parmesan cream sauce and prosciutto, topped off with the crisp sweetness of red grapes.

ENOUGH DOUGH FOR 1 PIZZA (SEE P 19)

1 tbsp/15 g butter

1 tbsp/7 g flour

1 cup/237 mL milk

¼ cup/45 g freshly grated Parmesan

¾ cup/90 g shredded mozzarella

3 oz/90 g prosciutto

¼ cup/30 g shelled pistachios, ground in a food processor or minced

1 cup/150 g red seedless grapes, quartered

2 oz/60 g crumbled blue cheese

Melt butter in a saucepan over medium high heat. Add flour and whisk until flour is incorporated and cooked. Slowly add milk, whisking as you go. Let milk simmer for 5 minutes. Remove from heat and add Parmesan.

Distribute mozzarella over dough. Drizzle sauce across the dough, starting at the outside closest to the crust and working toward the center. Layer the prosciutto over the sauce. Sprinkle with pistachio nuts. Bake in preheated oven at 500°F/260°C for 10–12 minutes until crust is golden brown. Sprinkle on grape quarters and blue cheese crumbles. Slice and serve.

BEET SPUNTINO

Spuntino is an Italian word that translates simply to mean "snack." And we like to think of this pizza as a full-blown snack attack. Roasted beets and potatoes make it filling, while the light grapefruit vinaigrette dressing adds a zesty dash of acidity. Pizza party tip: we make it vegan using a vegan cheese substitute or no cheese at all.

- -

ENOUGH DOUGH FOR 1 PIZZA (SEE P 19)

1 large beet, peeled and chopped

1½ lb/680 g blue potatoes, chopped (substitute fingerling potatoes depending on availability)

3 tbsp/44 mL olive oil

1 tsp salt

1 tsp pepper

1½ cups/355 mL marinara sauce (p 27)

1 cup/120 g shredded mozzarella cheese

½ cup/65 g raw red onions, sliced

½ cup/60 g chopped pecans

½ cup/75 g golden raisins

DRESSING (MAKES 2 PIES' WORTH)

½ cup/118 mL grapefruit juice (we use freshly squeezed for optimum flavor)

1 clove fresh garlic, chopped

½ tbsp/2 g oregano

½ tbsp/8 g salt

½ tbsp/6 g sugar

½ tbsp/4 g garlic powder

2 oz/59 mL red wine vinegar

½ cup/118 mL olive oil

Toss together diced beets and potatoes coated in olive oil, salt and pepper. Roast in preheated oven at 500°F/260°C for 25 minutes, or until beets and potatoes are tender. Let cool.

Combine all ingredients for dressing except for oil into food processor. While machine is running, slowly add olive oil in steady stream. Continue to blend until oil is fully coagulated. Separate the dressing in half and use half for the pizza and save half for a different yummy snack or for another pizza.

Apply marinara sauce and mozzarella. Spread potato and beet mixture evenly across cheese. Add red onions. Bake for 10–12 minutes in preheated oven at 500°F/260°C until crust is golden brown. Top with pecans, raisins and a light drizzle of dressing. Serve immediately. Note: wait to add dressing until you are ready to serve the pizza to avoid getting a soggy crust.

SALAD PIZZA

This is basically a salad in a glorified pizza crust bowl. We like to think of it as a dinner salad and main course all in one. We recommend substituting some of the fresh veggies on top for seasonal ingredients or any of your favorite dried or fresh fruits and vegetables. And on a personal note, Gurf, this one's for you. Just make sure you don't forget the kosher salt!

- -

ENOUGH DOUGH FOR 1 PIZZA (SEE P 19)

½ cup/60 g shredded mozzarella

2½ cups/90 g raw spinach

2 tbsp/30 mL olive oil

½ cup/65 g red onion, sliced

½ cup/80 g cherry tomatoes, halved

¼ cup/35 g kalamata olives, pitted and sliced

¼ cup/60 g artichoke hearts

3 tbsp/44 mL balsamic vinegar

A pinch of kosher salt

¼ cup/45 g Parmesan cheese, grated

Top the dough with mozzarella cheese and bake for 5–7 minutes in preheated oven at 500°F/260°C. Remove the pizza, but leave the oven on. Place spinach on top of the dough and drizzle olive oil over the spinach. It should look like too much spinach overflowing on the dough, but once it wilts it will shrink down significantly in size. Put the pizza back in the oven for an additional 3–5 minutes to wilt the spinach and until the crust is golden brown. Top with chopped vegetables in the order as they are listed. Drizzle balsamic vinegar over the vegetables, sprinkle kosher salt and finish with Parmesan cheese. Slice and serve.

RED, WHITE AND BERRY 'ZA

It doesn't get more patriotic than grilling. So why not jazz up the ingredients on your grill this summer? It's the land of the free for a reason. This dessert pizza mixes savory and sweet for an explosion in your mouth that beats bottle rockets and Pop Rocks any day. Recipe yields approximately two 12 inch/30.5 cm pizzas.

- -

ENOUGH DOUGH FOR 2 PIZZAS (SEE P 19)

2 cups/385 g sugar

2 cups/473 mL water

2 pt/1 L of fresh blueberries

¾ cup/25 g fresh mint leaves, finely shredded

1 lb/454 g fresh strawberries, stemmed and hulled

2 tsp/10 mL vegetable oil

12 fl oz/355 mL can condensed milk

¾ cup/90 g fresh ciliegine mozzarella, (small, cherry-sized) cut in half

Wooden skewers

Powdered sugar (optional for topping)

Combine sugar and water and bring to a boil. Pour the hot syrup over the blueberries and mint. Cool completely. This confit can be made up to a day in advance.

Toss strawberries lightly in vegetable oil. Place berries on skewers and grill until they blister slightly and start to soften, about 2 minutes. Remove the skewers and mash berries with a fork.

If you're making two pizzas, remember to split the ingredients equally between the pies for this part. Spread condensed milk across pizzas evenly. Evenly add dollops of the strawberry mash across the pies, then the fresh mozzarella and then the blueberry confit. Bake in preheated oven at 500°F/260°C for 10–12 minutes until crust is golden brown.

PIZZA PARTY TIP: Add an optional topping of powdered sugar.

THE CURE

Hangovers don't stand a chance against this recipe. In fact, we're not sure why it took us so long to realize this would make the perfect pizza. On a side note, this is the only pizza we included in this entire book that uses pepperoni (cue reactions of shock and awe!).

- -

ENOUGH DOUGH FOR 1 PIZZA (SEE P 19)

BLOODY MARY SAUCE

4¼ cups/1 L tomato juice

1 can (12 oz {340 g}) tomato paste

2 oz/60 mL Worcestershire sauce

2 oz/60 mL hot sauce,
we recommend Tabasco sauce

1 tbsp/15 g celery salt

Fresh ground pepper to taste

¾ cup/150 g sliced pepperoni

¼ cup/45 g green olives, halved

¼ cup/30 g celery, diced

1 cup/120 g shredded mozzarella

Chili salt

Combine all ingredients for Bloody Mary sauce in food processor and blend until smooth.

Apply Bloody Mary sauce the same way you apply marinara (p 27), and evenly add mozzarella on top. Distribute pepperoni, celery and green olives across pie. Bake for 10–12 minutes in preheated oven at 500°F/260°C or until crust is golden brown. Sprinkle chili salt lightly over pie. Slice and serve.

PIZZA PARTY TIP: The Bloody Mary mix yields enough to make a drink while you're cooking.

THE BBQ PORKABELLA

This pizza proves that slathered BBQ sauce provides the foundation for a meal to entice both your carnivorous and herbalicious friends. This is especially true when said BBQ sauce is made with a kick of your favorite porter beer. Plus, who doesn't like crispy wontons and cheddar cheese? This recipe will make approximately two 12 inch/30.5 cm pizzas.

- -

ENOUGH DOUGH FOR 2 PIZZAS (SEE P 19)

1½ lb/680 g pork shoulder

½ tbsp/8 g salt

Eight to ten 3" x 3"/8 x 8 cm wonton wrappers

3 cups/710 mL vegetable oil or enough to submerge the wonton strips for frying

4 portabella mushrooms, caps and stems cleaned and trimmed

4 fl oz/118 mL of your favorite porter beer, we suggest Revolution Brewery's Eugene Porter

¼ cup/59 mL BBQ sauce, we recommend Sweet Baby Ray's

½ cup/60 g mozzarella cheese, grated

½ cup/60 g cheddar cheese, grated

½ cup/25 g green onion, chopped

Rub pork shoulder with salt and place in a Dutch oven (or heavy oven-safe kettle) and bake in the oven at 325°F/163°C for 3 hours or until tender.

Prepare wontons (see p 34).

Toss portabellas lightly in oil and grill until tender and the mushrooms start to give off juice, about 4 minutes per side. Slice the stems in half and julienne. Cut the caps at a sharp thin angle on the bias, then julienne.

In a saucepan, stir in the beer with the BBQ sauce and simmer for 10 minutes. Let cool and set aside until you are ready to assemble the pizza.

If you're making two pizzas, use only half of your ingredients for this part. Apply rings of BBQ sauce evenly on pizza, starting at the crust and working inward toward center. Cover half the pie with the pulled pork and the other half with portabella strips. Add a line of BBQ sauce down the middle to designate each side clearly (your veggie friends will thank you for this). Top lightly with mozzarella and bake in preheated oven at 500°F/260°C for 10–12 minutes until crust is golden brown and cheese is melted. Upon removing the pizza from the oven, immediately add the grated cheddar, wontons and green onions (in that order) evenly. Let cheddar melt and serve with extra BBQ sauce for dipping and beers for drinking. Repeat this process for your second pizza.

BLUEBERRY CHIPOTLE FIGS

We have to admit: it wasn't until more recently that we learned figs existed (and are delicious!) in other forms outside of the Newton. This pizza plays the age-old sweet-against-spicy balancing act with the fiery zing of chipotle peppers mellowed out by the sweet blueberries and figs. Plus, it's way less healthy than a Fig Newton. Point for us!

- -

ENOUGH DOUGH FOR 1 PIZZA (SEE P 19)

½ pt/150 g fresh blueberries

3 oz/89 mL canned chipotle peppers in adobo sauce (careful, they are really hot!)

½ cup/60 g shredded mozzarella cheese

½ cup/118 mL BBQ sauce

1 cup/150 g dried mission figs

½ cup/145 g extra thick butcher-cut bacon, cooked and cut into small chunks

¼ cup/30 g shredded cheddar cheese

Place fresh blueberries and chipotle peppers in a small saucepan and cook together for 20 minutes over low heat, stirring regularly. Let cool. Purée with a food processor or blender until smooth and all large chunks are removed. Set aside until you are ready to assemble the pizza.

Add shredded mozzarella to the dough. Apply rings of BBQ sauce as the base of the pizza. Distribute dried figs and bacon. Bake for 10–12 minutes in preheated oven at 500°F/260°C until crust is golden brown. Add cheddar and let it melt on top. Drizzle with blueberry chipotle sauce and serve. This sauce is what we classify as "supah-dupah" spicy. Use with caution!

THE HULK

This mean and green pizza machine is packed with some of our favorite healthy snacks that just so happen to all be shades of green. And you know how we love that green (insert obligatory stoner joke here). Actually, we were talking about our rooftop garden filled with plentiful green ingredients we use on our pizzas. Recipe yields approximately two 12 inch/30.5 cm pizzas.

- -

ENOUGH DOUGH FOR 2 PIZZAS (SEE P 19)

3 Granny Smith apples
¾ cup/40 g green onions
3 tbsp/44 mL olive oil
1 cup/237 mL pesto (p 27)
1 cup/120 g shredded mozzarella
¾ cup/85 g pistachios, chopped

Core and hull the apples, halve them, coat lightly in olive oil and grill until skin blisters and the flesh side has grill marks. Let cool and then slice into small slivers.

Lightly coat onions in oil and grill on medium heat until the ends begin to char. Let cool and chop.

If you're making two pizzas, split the ingredients in half. Apply the pesto sauce gently onto the dough using a spatula. Distribute most of the mozzarella, followed by the apples and green onions evenly in that order. Sprinkle remaining pesto over the pie to help hold in moisture. Bake for 10–12 minutes in preheated oven at 500°F/260°C until crust is golden brown. Slice pizza as desired, and then add the pistachios on top of each slice before serving. Repeat this process for your second 'za.

BUY 10 SLICES
OR SALADS
AND THE 11TH
IS ON US.

Valid in-store for individual

dino's
'za piecycle

SRIRACHA HOT

DECON-STRUCTED DINER

As a late-night pizza joint, it seemed silly not to base at least some of our recipes off our favorite late-night-early-morning diner foods. There's something very timeless and nostalgic about diners. In many ways they're the epitome of American cuisine in its most unpretentious form. Oh, and it's delicious! Hearty soups, classic sandwiches, old-timey dinners and delectable breakfast sweets, what more could you need? There're also a few regional staples like Chicken 'n' Waffles and Skyline Chili.

And, as with any great diner, we have no shortage of wonderful and weird 3 a.m. stories. We've really seen it all. There was the time one of our employees got a Parmesan shaker thrown at his head because a customer wanted to get his attention (don't worry, he recovered fully). Then, on the opposite end of the spectrum, a certain employee received the tip of a midnight kiss from a complete stranger on New Year's Eve (apparently pizza is an aphrodisiac). And getting top billing, there was the time we got a glimpse of someone's University of Iowa Hawkeyes tattoo located on a cheek in a region of the body that should not be seen publicly (that's what skepticism gets you). There are other stories too...ones that should never see the light of day.

Though we can't guarantee that serving these pizzas from the safety of your own kitchen will result in stories as, uh, untamed as ours, it will re-create the best flavors of our favorite diner meals. But as a general rule of thumb, pizza served after midnight almost always comes with a good story.

STEAK 'N' EGGS

Forget Wheaties, this pizza is the true breakfast (or brunch) of champions. Flank steak, scrambled eggs and home fries all tied together with one very oversized slice of toast. Recipe yields two 12 inch/30.5 cm pizzas for extra-strength dining.

- -

ENOUGH DOUGH FOR 2 PIZZAS (SEE P 19)

GRILLED STEAK

2 flank steaks

2 tbsp/30 mL olive oil

2 tbsp/30 mL soy sauce

1 tsp salt

1 tsp pepper

HOME FRIES

8 red potatoes

1 tsp paprika

1 tsp cumin

1 tsp garlic powder

1 tsp salt

vegetable oil (just enough to cook the potatoes)

EGG MIXTURE

6 eggs

2 tbsp/6 g chives, chopped

1 tsp milk

½ tsp salt

½ tsp black pepper

½ tsp garlic powder

¼ cup/30 g shredded mozzarella

½ cup/60 g shredded cheddar

Hot sauce (optional, but we recommend Sriracha)

On a large cookie sheet, lay the steaks down flat in a single layer so that they are not overlapping. Apply a little bit of olive oil on each slice of steak. Rub the slices so that each one is covered by a thin layer of oil. Repeat this process with the soy sauce. Sprinkle a little bit of salt and pepper on each slice. Flip over each slice and add the oil, soy sauce, salt and pepper to the other side. Marinate in refrigerator for an hour.

Preheat grill on high. When the grill is hot, lay the steak flat on the grill. Using tongs, flip the steak on the grill until steak is cooked through on both sides. Let cool. Cut into small strips.

Submerge potatoes in large pot of water. Boil for 10–12 minutes until potatoes are tender. Cut potatoes into small cubes. Preheat pan with vegetable oil to 350°F/177°C. Submerge potatoes in frying oil until golden brown. Take out of pan and place on a paper towel. Toss with paprika, cumin, garlic powder and salt to taste.

Crack eggs into a bowl and whisk in chives, milk, salt, pepper and garlic. Fry in a frying pan until the mixture is cooked but a little bit runny.

If you're making two pies, don't forget to halve the ingredients equally between the two. Distribute shredded mozzarella on top of stretched dough. Add egg mixture, steak and home fries onto pizza in that order. Bake for 10–12 minutes in preheated oven at 500°F/260°C until crust is golden brown and cheese is melted. Add cheddar cheese and let melt.

PIZZA PARTY TIP: We always eat this pie with a drizzle of hot sauce on top; we recommend Sriracha.

DEVIL IN DISGUISE

Consider this a jazzed-up version of the favorite sandwich eaten by the King himself, Elvis Presley. And you'd better believe this is one hunka, hunka burning peanut-butter-bacon-banana love. Mandatory hip gyrations are required by all who enter the kitchen.

- -

ENOUGH DOUGH FOR 1 PIZZA (SEE P 19)

½ cup/60 g shredded mozzarella

1 cup/180 g smooth peanut butter

2 ripe bananas

3–5 strips of bacon, cooked

2 tbsp/30 mL honey (optional)

Top the dough crust with mozzarella cheese and bake for 5 minutes in preheated oven at 500°F/260°C. Remove pizza, but leave the oven on. Apply a generous layer of peanut butter to the base using a spatula. Slice the banana into small chunks and distribute across the pizza. Add bacon in strips across the pizza, or chop bacon and sprinkle it over the pizza. Bake for another 3–5 minutes. Drizzle honey on top and you're ready to get all shook up.

BISCUITS AND GROOVY

In the eternal words of Austin Powers, this pizza is "groovy, baby!" Your cardiologist may not share our sentiments here but hey, you only live once, baby! After all, not everyone gets the luxury of being brought back out of cryofreeze to resume life as a shagging, crime-fighting spy.

ENOUGH DOUGH FOR 1 PIZZA (SEE P 19)

SAUSAGE GRAVY

1 lb/454 g of ground sausage
¼ cup/60 g butter
½ cup/50 g flour
¾ tsp salt
½ tsp black pepper
½ qt/473 mL buttermilk

BISCUIT DOUGH

1½ cups/200 g Bisquick
¼ cup/59 mL buttermilk

½ cup/60 g shredded mozzarella
Freshly cracked black pepper

Brown sausage in a skillet on medium heat until cooked. Do not drain. Add butter and stir until melted. Then add flour, salt and pepper. Cook and stir constantly until flour begins to turn brown. Slowly add buttermilk while continuing to stir. Bring to a boil, then reduce to simmer for about 20 minutes or until consistency of gravy is reached. Remove from heat and set aside.

Combine ingredients for biscuits to form biscuit dough.

Top the dough crust with mozzarella cheese and bake for 5–7 minutes in preheated oven at 500°F/260°C. Remove the pizza, but leave the oven on. Spread sausage gravy across the crust using a spatula. Distribute mozzarella evenly. Break up biscuit dough into small chunks and evenly distribute across the pizza. Bake for another 5–7 minutes until crust and biscuits are golden brown. Crack fresh black pepper over pie and serve.

WELCOME TO THE TURKEY BACON CLUB

There's a reason that this sandwich is on just about every diner menu in existence, folks. Though we're pleased to say you won't need any of those little pointless colored toothpicks for this recipe. If it's not edible, keep it off the crust.

- -

**ENOUGH DOUGH FOR
1 PIZZA (SEE P 19)**

TURKEY

2 turkey legs

1 qt/945 mL turkey stock

2 sprigs of fresh rosemary

Salt and pepper

½ cup/118 mL mayonnaise

1 cup/120 g shredded mozzarella

3–4 strips of bacon, cooked and chopped

½ cup/80 g tomato, seeded and chopped

½ cup/20 g radish sprouts (any type will work though)

Place the turkey legs in a slow cooker with turkey stock, rosemary, salt and pepper to taste and cook on high for 3–4 hours. If you don't have a slow cooker, put the legs in a pan and roast in the oven at 350°F/177°C for 2–3 hours until tender and meat easily falls from the bone.

Once the meat is tender, remove from heat and let cool for about 15 minutes or until you can handle it. Shred the meat using two forks, careful to remove tendons and bones.

Bake crust in preheated oven at 500°F/260°C for 5–7 minutes. Remove pizza, but leave oven on. Spread mayo across the crust using a spatula. Lay slices of turkey folded in half over the entire pie, starting at the center and working toward the outside crust. Distribute mozzarella then bacon (in that order) over turkey slices. Bake for an additional 3–5 minutes until cheese is melted and crust is golden brown. Add tomatoes and radish sprouts. Slice and serve.

CHICKEN 'N' WAFFLES

Why this works, one may never know. But that it *does* work, no one will ever question. And because it was already the oh-so healthy combination of waffles, fried chicken, melted butter and syrup, we decided to add pizza crust and mozzarella cheese into the equation. Besides, this meal is way more fun to eat sans utensils (oh wait, that applies to most meals).

- -

ENOUGH DOUGH FOR 1 PIZZA (SEE P 19)

BREADED CHICKEN

½ cup/118 mL heavy cream

1 egg, beaten

1 tsp black pepper

½ tbsp/5 g fresh garlic, minced

1 tbsp/15 mL chicken base

½ tbsp/2 g fresh parsley, finely chopped

2 boneless, skinless chicken breasts, cut in half and then into strips

3 cups/710 mL vegetable oil for frying, or enough to submerge the chicken

Bread crumbs

WAFFLES

2 eggs

2 cups/200 g flour

1¾ cups/414 mL milk

1 tbsp/12 g white sugar

½ cup/118 mL vegetable oil

4 tsp/15 g baking powder

Pinch of salt

1 cup/120 g shredded mozzarella

¼ cup/60 mL melted butter

¼ cup/60 mL maple syrup (amount can vary depending on your taste)

Mix together heavy cream, eggs, black pepper, garlic, chicken base and parsley. Submerge chicken strips in mix and refrigerate overnight. If you're in a hurry, 2 hours will do. Sit out for about 10 minutes prior to cooking.

Heat oil to 350°F/177°C in large pan. Coat battered chicken in bread crumbs and then place them into hot oil. Check color every few minutes and rotate. When the tenders are a golden brown, pull out and place onto a paper towel-lined plate to soak up the grease. Let cool and then slice into ¼ inch/6 mm pieces.

Preheat the waffle iron. Beat the eggs until fluffy. Add the flour, milk, sugar, vegetable oil, baking powder and salt. Stir together but do not overmix.

Pour the mixture into the hot waffle iron. You can pretty much guarantee that the first waffle never looks as pretty as the others. Don't fret; it will taste just as delicious.

Continue until all the waffle batter is used up. Set the waffles aside to cool. Cut the waffles into small cubes. The size is up to you and dependent on the style of your waffle iron, but the important part is ensuring the waffle bites are all the same size for proper baking later.

Distribute shredded mozzarella, waffle bites and breaded chicken bites (in that order) across the dough. Bake in preheated oven at 500°F/260°C for 10–12 minutes until crust is golden brown. Drizzle melted butter and maple syrup and serve. This is the most important part: don't skimp on the butter and syrup!

TAKE
ANOTHER
LITTLE
PIZZA MY
HEART.
dimo's

THE GOVERNATOR BURGER PIZZA

A California-inspired burger jacked up with the meaty muscle of ground beef and pancetta. It even has a few delicious veggies on there. Just don't tell Arnold.

- -

ENOUGH DOUGH FOR 1 PIZZA (SEE P 19)

1 lb/454 g ground beef

3 tbsp/44 mL olive oil

1 tsp salt

1 tsp ground black pepper

½ tsp cayenne pepper

¼ cup/30 g shredded mozzarella

½ cup/118 mL Simple Cream sauce (p 26)

¼ cup/40 g tomatoes, chopped

¼ cup/33 g raw red onions, sliced

¼ lb/113 g pancetta arrotolata, cut in thinly sliced rounds and browned slightly for texture

6 oz/170 g goat cheese

¼ cup/15 g microgreens

Place goat cheese in freezer before starting preparation of the pizza. This will make assembling the pizza easier later.

Heat pan on medium and add ground beef, olive oil, salt, pepper and cayenne. Brown the meat thoroughly, stirring frequently. Let cool.

Evenly distribute shredded mozzarella. Apply rings of Simple Cream sauce, starting at the outside closest to the crust and working toward the center. Distribute ground beef. Bake in preheated oven at 500°F/260°C for 10–12 minutes until crust is golden brown. Top with chopped tomatoes, red onions and pancetta. Remove the goat cheese from the freezer, shred and distribute over the pie. Finish with microgreens. Slice and serve.

SKYLINE CHILI

Cincinnati's skyline may not be able to compete with Chicago's skyline (okay, so we're a little biased), but we have to give 'em the gold medal when it comes to their Skyline Chili. This recipe sticks to the authentic flavors of this Buckeye State classic, topped with melted cheddar and sour cream for a real pizza party in your mouth. The recipe makes two 12 inch/30.5 cm pizzas.

- -

ENOUGH DOUGH FOR 2 PIZZAS (SEE P 19)

CHILI

1 lb/454 g ground beef, run through the food processor

½ qt/473 mL water

1 cup/160 g tomato, crushed

1 white onion, finely chopped

1 tbsp/15 mL Worcestershire sauce

½ tbsp/5 g cocoa powder

2 tbsp/15 g chili powder

½ tsp cayenne

½ tsp red chili flakes

½ tsp cumin

1 tbsp/15 mL red wine vinegar

1 bay leaf

¼ tsp ground cloves

½ tsp cinnamon

¾ tsp salt

½ cup/118 mL sour cream

2 tbsp/30 mL heavy cream

½ whole white onion, finely chopped

1 cup/120 g shredded cheddar cheese

Combine all ingredients for chili into a large pot and simmer for 30 minutes.

Whisk sour cream and heavy cream together. Set aside until you are ready to assemble the pizza.

If you're making two pies, remember to split the ingredients equally between them during this part. Gently spread chili onto dough and evenly distribute over pie using a spatula. Careful not to puncture a hole into the dough. (Oh wait, too late? See tips for fixing holes, p 24) Distribute white onions over chili mixture. Bake in preheated oven at 500°F/260°C for 10–12 minutes until crust is golden brown. Add cheddar cheese and let melt. Apply sour cream rings, starting at the outside and working toward the center. Slice and serve.

FISH 'N' CHIPS

For this 'za, it's all about the tartar sauce, which creates a strong flavor base for fried tilapia and French fries, finished off with a dash of fresh squeezed lemon juice. Warning: lots of frying is about to take place. Substitute frozen French fries (thawed) if you must. This recipe makes approximately three 12 inch/30.5 cm pizzas or wrap some up and give to your neighbors.

- -

ENOUGH DOUGH FOR 3 PIZZAS (SEE P 19)

CHIPS

2 lb/434 g russet potatoes, cut into ¼"/6 mm spears

4 cups/946 mL frying oil (vegetable or peanut works for us)

Salt and pepper to taste

TILAPIA BEER BATTER

1½ cups/150 g flour

12 oz/355 mL can of beer

1 tsp baking powder

½ cup/118 mL milk

2 eggs

½ tsp seasoning, we suggest Old Bay

½ tsp salt

2 lb/434 g skinless and boneless tilapia, cut into strips

4 cups/946 mL frying oil (amount may vary depending on size of pan)

1 cup/100 g flour

1 tsp salt

1 tsp black pepper

TARTAR SAUCE

1 cup/237 mL mayonnaise

1 tbsp/15 mL sweet pickle relish

1 tbsp/5 g red onion, minced

1 tsp sugar

1 tsp lemon juice

Salt and pepper to taste

1½ cup/170 g shredded mozzarella

1-2 lemons, cut into wedges

Wash cut potatoes in cold running water and soak for about 1 hour in cold water—though longer (up to 24 hours in the refrigerator) is ideal. Pat dry thoroughly.

Heat first batch of oil for fries to 325°F/163°C in a large pot or Dutch oven, with enough oil to submerge potatoes with several inches of space left before the top of the pot (potatoes will boil over otherwise). Cook potatoes for about 5 minutes in the oil and remove. Set on a paper towel-lined plate to soak up excess oil. The potatoes will not be browned yet.

Turn the heat up on the oil to 400°F/204°C. Time to dip 'em in again for a second round of frying. This time keep the fries cooking in the oil until they're a nice golden brown shade. Again, remove and set on a paper towel-lined plate. Sprinkle with salt and pepper. Set aside to cool for later.

Mix all ingredients together for beer batter. Dip tilapia strips into batter and set aside for 10 minutes. Preheat vegetable oil to 375°F/191°C in a large pot, with enough oil to submerge tilapia strips. Combine flour, salt and pepper and dip battered tilapia strips into it. Place strips into hot oil. Cook until crispy and golden brown. Let cool and cut into small chunks.

Mix all ingredients for tartar sauce until well blended. Set aside until you are ready to assemble the pizza.

If you're making all three pizzas, remember to divide into thirds each ingredient during this part. Distribute mozzarella over dough. Apply rings of tartar sauce on top of mozzarella, starting at the outside closest to the crust and moving toward the center. Add crinkle-cut fries and pieces of fried fish. Bake in preheated oven at 500°F/260°C for 10-12 minutes until crust is golden brown. Top with freshly squeezed lemon juice. Slice and serve. Don't forget the extra tartar sauce for dipping and a pint to wash it all down.

GRILLED CHEESE WITH TOMATOES

They say not to mess with the classics, but sometimes we just can't help ourselves. Good ol' grilled cheese brings back memories of childhood, but now we've jazzed it up with three types of cheese and a pizza topper crust! Don't forget to add some tomato soup on the side for dipping.

- -

ENOUGH DOUGH FOR 2 PIZZAS (YOU'LL NEED ONE FOR THE TOPPER) (SEE P 19)

¾ cup/177 mL Simple Cream sauce (p 26)

½ cup/60 g shredded mozzarella

½ cup/60 g shredded gruyere

½ cup/60 g cheddar

1 large red tomato, sliced

2 tsp/5 g ground black pepper

Apply Simple Cream sauce in rings on dough crust, starting at the outside closest to the crust and working toward the center. Distribute shredded mozzarella, gruyere and cheddar evenly. Add slices of tomatoes evenly over the cheese. Sprinkle black pepper. Stretch out the extra dough into a thin layer without a crust. If you hold the dough up to a light it should look transparent. Lay it gently over the pizza. Cut slits into the dough to keep it from bubbling in the oven. Bake for 10–12 minutes in preheated oven at 500°F/260°C. Slice and serve.

FRENCH ONION SOUP

Bread bowls are so last week. But soup on a pizza? Can it be done? We suppose you'll just have to cook this recipe to find out for sure. You'll be such a soup trendsetter. Recipe yields approximately two 12 inch/30.5 cm pizzas worth of ingredients.

- -

ENOUGH DOUGH FOR 2 PIZZAS (SEE P 19)

SOUP SAUCE

2 tbsp/30 mL vegetable oil

2½ tbsp/15 g flour

1½ cup/354 mL beef broth

3 tbsp/44 mL dry white wine

2 cloves of garlic, minced

¼ tsp sugar

¼ tsp dried thyme

1 large white onion, sliced thinly

1 tsp olive oil

½ cup/118 mL water

1 tsp salt

CROUTONS

½ French baguette, cut into small cubes

4 tbsp/59 mL olive oil

1 tbsp/4 g parsley, finely chopped

1 tsp salt

1 tsp black pepper

1 tsp red pepper flakes

1 tsp dried oregano

¾ cup/90 g shredded gruyere cheese

Heat vegetable oil in a small pan over medium heat. Stir in flour using a fork and continue to stir until fully combined to create a roux. Using a fork to stir the mixture will help eliminate lumps. You want this to be a thick, smooth consistency that is light in color. When this is reached, remove from heat and let the mixture cool to room temperature.

In a large saucepan, combine beef broth, dry white wine, garlic, sugar and thyme. Bring to a boil. Turn down heat and stir in roux mixture. Simmer over low heat, stirring regularly, until the mixture thickens to the consistency of gravy. Let cool.

Add onions with oil and salt in a pan and heat on medium. Stir in water. Cook until water evaporates and the onions turn a deep brown color. Set aside to cool.

Cover cubes of French bread in oil and mix with seasonings. Bake on a cookie sheet in preheated oven at 425°F/218°C until bread gets crispy and browns. This should only take about 5–7 minutes. Let cool.

If you're making two pies, remember to split the ingredients equally between the two during this part. Spread the soup sauce mixture generously over dough. Add onions and shredded gruyere. Bake in preheated oven at 500°F/260°C for 10–12 minutes until crust is golden brown. Top with croutons and optional additional shredded cheese. Slice and serve.

RODEO BURGER

This is a loose take on our favorite slice from Boss Lady Pizza, our sister company from another (very bossy) mother, located in Boulder, Colorado. This recipe for French fried onions will make you weak in the knees. Seriously. We boosted the yield a bit for you to munch on them while the 'za bakes. And if you're ever in Boulder, don't miss Boss Lady Pizza...and ask for extra bossy sauce on the side.

- -

ENOUGH DOUGH FOR 1 PIZZA (SEE P 19)

2 flank steaks
Soy sauce, to taste
Worcestershire sauce, to taste
Salt and pepper, to taste

FRENCH FRIED ONION STRINGS

2 to 3 large yellow onions

2 cups/475 mL of buttermilk

2 cups/200 g of flour

½ tsp of cayenne pepper

1 tbsp/15 g of salt

1 tbsp/8 g black pepper

2 qt/1.89 L of canola oil (enough to submerge onions for frying)

¾ cup/177 mL BBQ sauce, we recommend Sweet Baby Ray's

½ cup/60 g shredded mozzarella cheese

½ cup/60 g shredded cheddar cheese

The steaks should be thinly cut (they normally come this way from the butcher ¼ inch "{6 mm}). Grill steaks on an actual grill, or in a frying pan if in a pinch, with a dash of soy sauce, Worcestershire sauce, salt and pepper. Cook to medium. Set aside for later.

Slice the onions into very thin rings. It's important to slice the onion rings to a thickness of ⅛ inch/3.2 mm. If too thick, they will become somewhat soggy after they are fried. Use a mandolin slicer for this if you have one. Soak the sliced onions in the buttermilk for at least an hour. We add a dash of black pepper to this mix also for an extra flavor boost. Mix together the flour, cayenne, salt, pepper and set aside.

After the onions have soaked in the buttermilk, run them through the flour mixture. Be sure to completely coat the onions in the mixture. Shake off any excess flour before adding to the oil.

Heat canola oil to 375°F/191°C in a large pan. Add the coated onions to oil and cook until golden brown, usually about 5 minutes.

Apply rings of BBQ sauce to dough, starting at the outside closest to the crust and working toward the center. Add shredded mozzarella and strips of steak. Bake in preheated oven at 500°F/260°C for 10–12 minutes until crust is golden brown. Top with French fried onions and cheddar. Let cheese melt, slice and serve.

CELIA'S SWEET PEACH COBBLER

This slice is named for a former employee who can be credited with its sugary sweet creation. In fact, Celia created many of our delectable specials over the years (Chicken 'n' Waffles, anyone?), but this one will always be our favorite. It will probably soon be your favorite, too. From our experiences, it's even better when brought for dessert on a summer's day picnic in the park. This recipe yields enough ingredients to bake 2 pies. Share the love.

- -

ENOUGH DOUGH FOR 2 PIZZAS (SEE P 19)

SWEET PEACHES

7 peaches, cut into slices
½ cup/95 g sugar
1 tbsp/15 mL lemon juice
½ cup/118 mL apple juice
1 tsp cinnamon
1 tbsp/7 g tapioca flour

BISCUITS

1 cup/130 g Bisquick
¼ cup/59 mL milk
1½ tbsp/20 g sugar

1 cup/120 g shredded mozzarella
(½ cup {60 g} per pizza)

Put peaches in a saucepan and add sugar, lemon and apple juice, cinnamon and tapioca flour. Bring to boil and then simmer until peaches are cooked and syrup is thick.

Combine all ingredients for biscuits to form dough. Do not overmix.

Using a spatula, gently spread peach mixture onto dough. Distribute shredded mozzarella. Spoon out small chunks of biscuit dough onto the pizza to create mini biscuit shapes. Bake in preheated oven at 500°F/260°C for 10–12 minutes until crust is golden brown. Slice and serve.

COMFORT CRAVINGS

Can you remember your first slice of pizza? There's a pretty good chance that it was delivered to your front door and eaten on your couch with a paper plate. No, it wasn't extravagant. Nonetheless it felt, as we remember it, like the definition of comfort food.

These days, 'za has become synonymous with nostalgic memories like that for us. Come to think of it, there are quite a few meals that have that effect on us. There are the mashed potatoes, steaming hot with melted butter and garlic. Then there is always the home-style mac 'n' cheese like Mom baked in the oven with oversized elbow noodles. There's the crispy, sizzling bacon and sweet drizzled syrup. And pretty much anything else fried or with melted cheese on top.

This chapter will prove that you can have your pizza and eat the mashed potatoes, too. The only thing more gratifying than your favorite comfort food is all your favorite comfort foods on one doughy plate. Whether you want to relive your favorite childhood meals, create new delicious memories or just get comfy on the couch, these pizzas will fill your most shameless cravings.

SMACK 'N' CHEESE

We turned up the heat on our infamous fan favorite: The Mac 'n' Cheese pizza. Chipotle peppers and grilled jalapeños harmonize with the oh-so-decadent comfort of cheesy macaroni noodles. No further introduction needed. Recipe yields two 12 inch/30.5 cm pizzas.

- -

ENOUGH DOUGH FOR 2 PIZZAS (SEE P 19)

SMACK SAUCE

1 large jalapeño, roasted, peeled and chopped

1 (13.5 oz {399 mL}) can of chipotle peppers in adobo sauce

2 cups/473 mL heavy cream

¼ cup/30 g shredded cheddar cheese

¼ cup/20 g Parmesan cheese

½ tsp salt

½ tsp ground black pepper

2 cups/230 g of cooked, drained and cooled macaroni elbow noodles

¼ cup/30 g shredded hot pepper cheese

Combine ingredients for smack sauce in a saucepan and simmer over low heat for 10 minutes, or until the sauce becomes smooth and the cheese melts completely. Toss with macaroni noodles.

If you're making two pizzas, remember to split the ingredients equally for this part. Use a spatula to spread the noodles and sauce mixture in an even layer across the dough. Grate the hot pepper cheese on top of the noodle mixture, evenly spread from the center of dough to the crust. Bake pizza in preheated oven at 500°F/260°C for 10–12 minutes until the crust is golden and the cheese is completely melted. Let cool for about 5 minutes to allow cheese sauce to thicken up.

PIZZALOSOPHY 101: This is only the beginning of the Mac Revolution. Turns out macaroni noodles and pizza crust make a pretty unstoppable team. Other delectable ingredients to pair with your Mac Pizza include shredded beef, bacon (obviously), smoked cheese, grilled seasonal veggies and even truffle cream for the foodie mac lovers out there. Experiment. You already broke the rules by putting noodles on a pizza. So why not go a little crazy?

CHEESY POTATO

Much like macaroni noodles, potatoes can be combined with cheese, crust and additional toppings in many different combinations. This recipe provides a delicious base that's perfect for adding extra flavor boosters like chives with cracked black pepper or jalapeños with bacon.

- -

ENOUGH DOUGH FOR 1 PIZZA (SEE P 19)

½ cup/118 mL sour cream

2 tbsp/30 mL heavy cream

5 medium Yukon gold potatoes

½ cup/60 g shredded mozzarella cheese

½ cup/60 g shredded cheddar cheese

½ cup/60 g shredded Asiago cheese

CHOICE OF:

½ cup/25 g of chopped chives and 2 tbsp/12 g cracked black pepper

OR

3-4 strips cooked and chopped bacon and 2 jalapeños, seeded and sliced

Mix sour cream with heavy cream until it's approximately the consistency of buttermilk. Keep refrigerated until you're ready to assemble the pizza.

Clean the potatoes. Boil potatoes, being careful not to overcrowd the pot and cause it to boil over. Boil until soft. Drain the water and put potatoes aside to cool. Once cooled, slice into ¼ inch/6 mm rounds.

Apply sour cream mixture in rings, starting at the crust and working toward the center. Distribute shredded mozzarella. Add sliced potatoes in a single layer over the top. Bake in preheated oven at 500°F/260°C for 10–12 minutes until golden brown. Top with cheddar and Asiago immediately out of the oven and let cheese melt. Top with additional finishing ingredients of your choice. Slice and serve.

SCHMALTZ SUPREME

Sometimes you just need to slow down and let the schmaltz (aka fat) do the cooking for you because you can't rush tender, meaty goodness. Slow-roasted chicken pairs with a rich butter and schmaltz sauce, accompanied by petite roasted pearl onions and smoked Gouda. The result: French bistro meets your momma's Crock-Pot. Recipe yields approximately two 12 inch/30.5 cm pizzas worth of ingredients.

- -

ENOUGH DOUGH FOR 2 PIZZAS (SEE P 19)

4 garlic cloves, peeled

2 shallots, peeled

1 tsp dried sage

½ tsp dried marjoram

½ tsp dried thyme

½ tsp dried rosemary

1 tbsp/15 g salt (and a little extra for the onions later)

1 tbsp/8 g coarse ground black pepper

¼ cup/59 mL chicken gravy

1 stick unsalted butter, softened at room temperature

4–6 chicken pinwheels (leg and thigh together), rinsed and patted dry

2 tbsp/13 g all-purpose flour

2 cups/473 mL heavy cream

1 tbsp/3 g fresh chives, chopped

16 oz/254 g bag frozen pearl onions

1 tsp vegetable oil

2 cups/230 g smoked Gouda

Place the garlic and shallots in a large food processor and pulse until both are finely chopped. Add sage, marjoram, thyme, rosemary, salt, pepper and butter to the food processor and pulse until they are fully incorporated and the butter has taken on a smooth and even consistency. Coat the chicken legs with the butter mixture.

Place the chicken legs along with the remaining butter in a heavy-bottomed roasting pan and cover tightly with foil. Bake at 350°F/177°C for 1 hour, or until an internal temperature of the chicken reaches 165°F/74°C. Remove the chicken from the pan drippings and allow the legs to cool. Remove the chicken skins and pull the meat from the cooled legs. Shred the dark meat by hand, or chop roughly with a chef knife.

Add flour to the pan drippings and stir over low heat until the flour has been fully absorbed. Add heavy cream and simmer until the pan drippings and cream have become a smooth sauce, then remove from heat and add chives. Let cool and set aside until you are ready to assemble the pizza.

Toss the pearl onions with vegetable oil and a pinch of salt. Bake at 450°F/232°C for 20 minutes, or until the onions have charred to a medium brown.

If you're making two pies, remember to split the ingredients equally for this part. Apply rings of the sauce consistently across the dough. Add the shredded chicken generously over sauce. Grate smoked Gouda over chicken. Bake in preheated oven at 500°F/260°C for 10–12 minutes until crust is golden brown. Garnish with extra chives.

MOMMA'S MEATLOAF

We're not sure about you, but this is one of those dishes growing up that always, well, scared us a bit. But in our older and wiser years, we've come to embrace the meaty goodness of the loaf. So, without further ado, this one's for you, Mom (this recipe actually belongs to an employee's mom, so you know it's legit!).

ENOUGH DOUGH FOR 1 PIZZA (SEE P 19)

MEAT LOAF MIXTURE

1½ lb/680 g ground beef

½ lb/227 g ground sausage

1½ cup/355 mL ketchup

½ cup/118 mL Worchestershire sauce

1 tsp hot sauce, we suggest using Tabasco sauce

1 egg

1½ cup/120 g rolled oats

1½ celery stalks, finely chopped

½ cup/75 g white onion, finely chopped

Salt and pepper

¾ cup/90 g shredded mozzarella

BBQ sauce and ketchup for topping

Mix all ingredients for the meat loaf mixture together and spread out onto a cookie sheet. Bake in preheated oven at 375°F/190°C for 30–45 minutes or until the mixture browns. Do not overcook! Remember, it still has to go back in the oven on the pizza. Let the mixture cool for about 15 minutes before assembling the pizza.

Spread a small amount of the shredded mozzarella to the dough. Apply rings of BBQ sauce, starting at the outside closest to the crust and working toward the center. Follow with crumbled meat loaf bites, distributing the meat evenly across the dough. Top with remaining shredded mozzarella. Bake in preheated oven at 500°F/260°C for 10–12 minutes until crust is golden brown. Apply rings of ketchup immediately out of the oven. Slice and serve. Make mom proud and serve it with some veggies on the side.

BROCCOLI BACON MASHER

Nothing announces the arrival of autumn like the falling of leaves, the chill of Chicago wind on your cheeks and the warmth of Broccoli Bacon Masher pizza baking in the oven. A slice of this 'za and we'll valiantly take on any cold weather the Windy City throws at us. That, or we'll settle into the couch for a nap. We consider it a win either way. Recipe yields approximately three 12 inch/30.5 cm pizzas.

- -

ENOUGH DOUGH FOR 3 PIZZAS (SEE P 19)

3 lb/1.36 kg Yukon gold potatoes
½ lb/226 g butter
1 cup/240 mL heavy cream
½ cup/90 g Parmesan cheese
1 head broccoli
1 tbsp/10 g fresh garlic, minced
½ cup/140 g bacon, cooked and chopped
1 cup/120 g cheddar cheese
Freshly ground black pepper and salt

Clean the potatoes. Place potatoes into the pot and boil until soft, being careful not to overcrowd the pot to avoid it boiling over. Once soft (check with a fork), strain out the water and mash with butter, heavy cream and Parmesan cheese. The consistency should be more like a thick sauce so that it's easy to apply to the pizza dough.

Cut and discard broccoli stem. Cut florets into bite-size pieces and steam. Salt to taste.

If you're making all three pies, remember to share the ingredients equally on each. Spread the potato mixture so there is a ¼ inch/6 mm layer across the entire dough crust. Evenly distribute broccoli florets, bacon and cheddar cheese. Bake in preheated oven at 500°F/260°C for 10–12 minutes until the crust is golden brown and the cheese is melted. Add freshly cracked black pepper to taste.

BEEF STROGANOFF

This hearty dish is best served to help fight off the very-cold-weather blues. No, we're not talking about the first day it gets below freezing. We're talking about mid-January when you're wearing five layers of sweaters just to leave the house. That is likely why this meal was created in 19th-century Russia. If you live in a warm weather climate, you'll just have to use your imagination. Recipe yields approximately three 12 inch/30.5 cm pizzas.

- -

ENOUGH DOUGH FOR 3 PIZZAS (SEE P 19)

BEEF

3 lb/1.5 kg beef brisket

16 fl oz/475 mL beef broth

1 cup/240 mL of water

3 tbsp/45 mL soy sauce

2 cloves garlic, chopped

SAUCE

1 cup/75 g button mushrooms, finely chopped

1 tsp fresh garlic, minced

2 tsp/6 g white onion, finely chopped

2 cups/480 mL beef stock (from the chuck roast)

1 tbsp/15 g butter

2 cups/480 mL heavy cream

CARAMELIZED ONIONS

1 large white onion, sliced thinly

2 tsp/10 mL olive oil

Salt

½ cup/120 mL water

2 cups/180 g egg noodles

Salt

1 cup/120 g shredded mozzarella

1 tbsp/2.5 g fresh parsley, finely chopped

Combine ingredients for brisket in a roasting pan and marinate overnight in the refrigerator. Cover with aluminum foil and bake in preheated oven at 300°F/149°C for about 3 hours, or until the meat is tender and breaks apart with fork. Let cool and shred beef.

Sauté all ingredients for sauce except for heavy cream. Add heavy cream and simmer until soup thickens to the consistency of gravy. Let cool and set aside until you are ready to assemble the pizza.

Add onions and olive oil with a dash of salt in pan over low heat. Stir in water and cook until water evaporates and the onions take on a deep brown color. Let cool and toss onions with the cooked and shredded beef.

Boil egg noodles in salted water, drain and shock in cold water.

If you're making all three pies, remember to split the ingredients equally during this part. Apply mozzarella cheese to the dough, but only enough so that you'll have an equal amount to apply again later. Evenly distribute egg noodles, followed by the beef and onion mixture. Top with rings of mushroom sauce, starting at the outside and working toward the center. Add remaining mozzarella. Bake in preheated oven at 500°F/260°C for 10–12 minutes until crust is golden brown and cheese is melted. Top with fresh parsley, slice and serve.

THANKSGIVING LEFTOVERS PIE

This slice takes all the ingredients you already have in your fridge post-Turkey Day and makes 'em into a pie (as if you didn't already know that from the name). Because you can only eat so many cold turkey sandwiches after Thanksgiving before getting sick (by our count it's about eight sandwiches). And if you get a craving mid-May for Thanksgiving dinner, we won't judge if you make this from scratch.

ENOUGH DOUGH FOR 1 PIZZA (SEE P 19)

¾ cup/160 g mashed potatoes (if you don't have a recipe, ours is on p 82)

½ lb/225 g shredded turkey meat

½ cup/60 g shredded mozzarella

¾ cup/120 g stuffing

½ cup/120 mL gravy (if you need a recipe for this, ours is below)

¼ cup/30 g dried cranberries

MUSHROOM GRAVY RECIPE

(you only need this if you don't already have one for the ½ cup of gravy above)

½ lb/230 g white mushrooms

½ white onion

1 tbsp/10 g fresh garlic, minced

1 tbsp/15 g butter

½ tbsp/8 mL soy sauce

¼ cup/60 mL sherry

½ tbsp/8 mL balsamic vinegar

2 cups/475 mL chicken stock

½ tsp sugar

If you need a gravy recipe, here are the directions for ours. If you have your own, go on and do your thing, friend! We'll catch up with you in the next paragraph. Chop mushrooms and onions. Cook garlic in butter for a few minutes. Add onions and cook until soft. Add mushrooms and soy sauce and cook until mushrooms are browned. Add sherry and vinegar and cook until liquid evaporates. Add chicken stock and sugar and cook for another couple of minutes. Let cool. Blend in food processor until gravy is smooth.

Apply the mashed potatoes gently to the dough using a spatula, careful not to puncture a hole in the dough. Distribute turkey meat evenly, and top with shredded mozzarella. Bake in preheated oven at 500°F/260°C for 10 minutes. Remove pizza, but leave oven on. Top with stuffing and drizzle gravy over pizza. Heat in oven for additional 3–5 minutes, careful not to overcook the bottom of the pizza. Finish with dried cranberries, slice and serve. No carving of the turkey required.

THE STONER KID

All clichés aside, we are a pizza joint, and we've employed our fair share of stoner kids. Grateful Dead and Phish playlists aplenty, we've also gotten some pretty good fully "baked" ideas as a result. This pie is one of them. It sounds strange but, even fully sober, we think you'll enjoy this unsuspecting mashup of flavors.

- -

ENOUGH DOUGH FOR 1 PIZZA (SEE P 19)

1 cup/200 g French fries (to make your own, see p 105)

¼ cup/60 mL Simple Cream sauce (p 26)

½ cup/85 g jalapeños, seeded and diced

1 cup/120 g cheddar cheese

2 tbsp/30 mL honey

If you've used frozen French fries, let them thaw for about 20 minutes at room temperature. Apply Simple Cream onto dough in rings using a spoon. There should be just enough sauce to lightly cover the dough. Evenly distribute the French fries over the sauce. Sprinkle diced jalapeños evenly across the pie. Repeat this same step with the cheddar cheese. Bake in preheated oven at 500°F/260°C for 10–12 minutes until crust is golden brown and cheese is melted. Drizzle honey over the pizza before serving.

BUILD ME UP, BUTTERNUT

Let's set the ideal scene for you to best enjoy this slice. It's mid-October—you're sipping some hot apple cider (or, let's be real, maybe it's a pumpkin ale) and the inebriating aromas of rosemary, sage and thyme are wafting through the kitchen. Now doesn't that sound magical? Yep, this is a pie sure to build you up, but never let you down. This recipe makes approximately two 12 inch/30.5 cm pizzas.

ENOUGH DOUGH FOR 2 PIZZAS (SEE P 19)

GRILLED CHICKEN

2 chicken breasts

¾ cup/180 ml white vinegar

1 cup/240 mL olive oil (plus a little extra for the dough)

½ cup/20 g fresh basil, chopped finely

½ tbsp/8 mL salt

½ tbsp/5 g fresh garlic

¼ cup/10 g fresh parsley, chopped finely

6 oz/120 g loaf of goat cheese

SQUASH PURÉE

1 small butternut squash

2 tsp/10 mL olive oil

Salt to taste

Pepper to taste

2 tbsp/20 g fresh garlic, diced

2-4 leaves of fresh sage

2 sprigs of fresh rosemary

2 sprigs of fresh thyme

1 cup/240 mL vegetable broth

Rub chicken with dry ingredients and then place in a pan to marinate in the wet ingredients in the refrigerator overnight.

When your chicken is marinated and you're ready to start cooking, place the goat cheese in the freezer. It'll make it easy to cut it later.

Cut squash in half lengthwise. Remove seeds with a spoon. Rub halves with olive oil, salt and pepper. Take garlic, sage, rosemary and thyme and place in each squash cavity. Place in roasting dish skin side down, cover with aluminum foil and roast at 350°F/177°C for 1 hour or until the squash is tender (use a fork to test it). Let cool, then spoon out squash and herbs from rind into food processor and add broth. Purée until smooth.

Preheat grill or nonstick pan on medium-high. When grill is hot, lay chicken breasts flat on the grill. Flip the chicken and keep it over the heat until it's cooked through. Let chicken cool. Cut into small strips.

If you're making two pies, remember to equally split the ingredients during this part. Drizzle a very small amount of olive oil on the dough and parbake the crust in preheated oven at 500°F/260°C for 5–7 minutes. Remove the pizza, but leave the oven on. Spread butternut purée evenly across the crust. Place grilled chicken strips on the purée. Remove the goat cheese from the freezer and shred and distribute over the grilled chicken. Place pizza back in the oven for another 5 minutes until crust is golden and cheese melts. Slice and serve.

BURNHARD

A little bit sweet, a little bit spicy, a lotta bit meaty. BBQ slathered chuck roast beef finished with the smoky heat of grilled jalapeños and fiery finish of hot sauce. It burns so good.

- -

ENOUGH DOUGH FOR 1 PIZZA (SEE P 19)

1½ lb/680 g chuck beef
1 tbsp/15 mL salt
4–6 jalapeños
BBQ sauce
Hot sauce, we suggest Sriracha
½ cup/60 g shredded mozzarella

Place beef in a large pot and fill with water to cover. Simmer with salt until tender and meat breaks apart with a fork. Once cooled, shred with fingers.

Grill whole jalapeños in oil on medium-hot heat until skin blisters. Let cool. Peel, remove seeds and chop finely.

Combine beef and jalapeños. Toss with BBQ sauce to cover meat.

Apply rings of BBQ sauce on dough, starting at the outside closest to the crust and working toward the center. Spread most of the mozzarella over sauce. Add the beef and jalapeño mixture to the pizza. Top with additional mozzarella. Bake in preheated oven at 500°F/260°C until crust is golden brown. Top with Sriracha sauce rings, slice and serve.

PUMPKIN PIE

It's not autumn without the unavoidable pumpkin craze. Pumpkin spice this, pumpkin flavored that. Well, not to sound overly confident here, but those are all just opening acts compared to this 'za. It's pizza and pie all in one. Bring this one to the family Thanksgiving to amaze the in-laws. This recipe yields approximately two 12 inch/30.5 cm pizzas.

- -

ENOUGH DOUGH FOR 2 PIZZAS (SEE P 19)

PUMPKIN SAUCE

1 small pumpkin

Olive oil (just enough to coat the pumpkin)

2 large eggs

½ cup/120 mL heavy whipping cream

½ cup/100 g light brown sugar

1 tsp ground cinnamon

½ tsp ground ginger

⅛ tsp ground cloves

½ tsp salt

1½ cups/75 g mini-marshmallows

1 cup/120 g chopped pecans

Chocolate sauce (optional)

Whipped cream(optional)

Quarter pumpkin and coat sections in a small amount of olive oil. Place in roasting dish skin side down, cover with aluminum foil and roast in preheated oven at 350°F/177°C for 1 hour or until fork tender. Let cool.

Scoop softened pumpkin into food processor and purée.

Combine with other ingredients for the pumpkin sauce and mix until fully combined. Should be about the consistency of gravy.

If you're making two pizzas, remember to divide the ingredients equally between them for this part. Apply pumpkin purée gently to the dough using a spatula, careful not to apply too much pressure to avoid puncturing the dough. Cover pumpkin sauce evenly with mini-marshmallows, followed by pecans. Bake in preheated oven at 500°F/260°C for 10–12 minutes until crust is golden brown and marshmallows expand and brown. Drizzle with optional chocolate sauce or serve with whipped cream.

MAIN COURSE MEALS

Queue the music, dim the lights and please, hold the applause until the end of the show. These pies are the sultry and harmonious headlining acts. They take rule breaking to the next level of deliciousness. Planning a romantic date? Need to impress the boss with an unforgettable dinner party? Reminiscing about that trip you took to (insert cool vacation locale here)? You'll find a 'za for all these occasions here.

DIMO THE GREEK

Fresh mint combined with delicate pieces of tender leg of lamb and potatoes with garlic. The classic flavors in this dish result in a beautiful and aromatic meal sure to impress diners. If you're going to classify a pizza as "high class," this would be the one.

ENOUGH DOUGH FOR 1 PIZZA (SEE P 19)

COMPOUND BUTTER

1 tsp garlic
½ cup/115 g butter
3 shallots
1 tsp salt
1 tsp pepper
¼ cup/60 mL Riesling wine
1 tsp lemon juice

1 lamb shank

AU JUS SAUCE

Cooking juices from lamb and butter
3 tbsp/18 g flour
3 tbsp/45 mL water

4–5 Yukon Gold potatoes
2 cloves garlic, smashed
Salt and pepper to taste
1 tbsp/15 g butter

¾ cup/180 mL marinara sauce (p 27)
¾ cup/90 g shredded mozzarella
Fresh mint leaves (enough to cover the pie with the leaves)

Combine all ingredients for compound butter in food processor. Spread the butter over the lamb and place in roasting pan. Roast the lamb at 450°F/232°C in preheated oven for approximately 20 minutes to brown. Then, turn the heat down to 400°F/204°C and cook for an additional 40-50 minutes until an internal temperature of 135°F/57°C is reached. Cool for about 10 minutes then slice.

Mix together flour and water for au jus sauce in a saucepan until combined. Stir in juices from lamb and butter. Reduce to low heat until color is shiny.

Cut potatoes into wedges and combine with garlic, salt, pepper and butter in a roasting dish. Cover and bake at 425°F/218°C until potatoes are tender and browned—about 15 minutes. Let cool.

Apply marinara sauce to dough (see tips, p 28). Distribute shredded mozzarella, followed by lamb slices and potatoes and garlic. Top with a drizzle of au jus sauce. Bake in preheated oven at 500°F/260°C until crust is golden brown. Top with mint leaves. Slice and serve.

ENCASED MEATS

You can't go wrong with sausage pizza. Some of our favorites include andouille, turducken, kielbasa or good old classic Italian sausage (even better if it's spicy). Though our pizzas are more often labeled "crazy" or "unbelievable," we can't forget the staples. This pizza is simple, but highly effective in the flavor department.

- -

ENOUGH DOUGH FOR 1 PIZZA (SEE P 19)

3 types of sausage links (¼ lb {115 g} of each type)

1 cup/240 mL marinara (p 27)

½ cup/60 g shredded mozzarella

½ cup/60 g finely grated pecorino

¼ cup/10 g fresh parsley, finely chopped

Grill the sausage until cooked through and browned on the outside. Slice all sausages in half lengthwise and then slice into thin half-moons. Mix sausages together in a large bowl to get a good variety when spread out on the pie.

Apply marinara and shredded mozzarella evenly on the pie. Distribute sausage pieces across cheese. Bake in a preheated oven at 500°F/260°C for 10–12 minutes until crust is golden brown. Top with pecorino and parsley. Slice and serve.

JAMAICAN JERK CHICKEN

Feel the rhythm! Feel the rhyme! Get on up, it's bobsled...uh, we mean chicken...time! This pie features a traditional Jamaican jerk marinade with a fiery zing that's not quite *Cool Runnings*, but definitely unforgettable. This recipe makes approximately two 12 inch/30.5 cm pizzas.

- -

ENOUGH DOUGH FOR 2 PIZZAS (SEE P 19)

CHICKEN MARINADE

¼ cup/25 g green onions

½ cup/43 g white onion, finely chopped

1 tbsp/4 g fresh thyme, chopped

2 tbsp/25 g brown sugar, tightly packed

2 tsp/4 g allspice

1 tsp nutmeg

1 tsp cayenne pepper

1 tsp grated ginger

½ tsp ground black pepper

2 tbsp/30 mL olive oil

½ cup/120 mL orange juice

½ cup/120 mL soy sauce

¼ cup/60 mL white vinegar

1 Scotch bonnet pepper, seeded and chopped (don't forget to wear gloves!)

3 skinless and boneless chicken breasts, halved

1 large green pepper

½ cup/75 g white onion, sliced

½ cup/120 mL Simple Cream sauce (p 26)

1 cup/120 g shredded mozzarella

1 cup/230 mL pineapple chunks, drained

Mix all ingredients together for marinade in food processor until smooth. Fill two large plastic bags with chicken and split marinade between the two bags. Marinate overnight.

Preheat grill on high then lower heat to medium range once hot. Cook chicken on both sides until browned—about 25–30 minutes. Slice the green pepper into strips. Then, toward the end of cooking, add the green pepper and onions on to the grill and cook until browned.

If you're making two pies, don't forget to split the ingredients equally between them during this part. Apply Simple Cream sauce in rings onto the dough. Add most of the shredded mozzarella, then chicken, pepper and onions. Top with additional mozzarella. Bake in preheated oven at 500°F/260°C for 10–12 minutes until crust is golden brown. Top with pineapple chunks. Slice and serve.

FALAFEL PIZZA

Sometimes inspiration for pizzas comes when we least expect it. This time we were mid-construction on our second location. It had been a very long and exhausting day finalizing plans for the decor of the dining room. We were starving. The closest place was a Chicago favorite for Middle Eastern cuisine, with possibly the best falafel in the city. It was that night, amid the freshly cut wood for tables and booths and the newly painted walls of the still unfinished second store, that we knew there must be a falafel pizza. Recipe makes approximately two 12 inch/30.5 cm pizzas.

- -

ENOUGH DOUGH FOR 2 PIZZAS (SEE P 19)

FALAFEL BALLS

16 oz/454 g can of chickpeas, drained

¼ cup/40 g white onion, finely chopped

1 tsp cumin

1 tsp coriander

1 tsp garlic, minced

½ tsp salt

2 tbsp/6 g chives, chopped

1½ tbsp/9 g all-purpose flour

3 cups/710 mL vegetable oil for frying

HUMMUS SAUCE

16 oz/454 g can of chickpeas

½ cup/118 mL juice from the chickpea can

3 tbsp/45 mL lemon juice

2 tbsp/30 mL olive oil

2 tbsp/30 mL tahini

2 cloves of garlic

VEGETABLE MIX

3–4 Roma tomatoes, seeded and chopped

1 cucumber, peeled, seeded and chopped

½ white onion, chopped

¼ cup flat-leaf parsley, chopped

1 tbsp/15 mL olive oil

1 tsp paprika (plus a little extra)

Salt and pepper to taste

½ cup/60 g shredded mozzarella

Place drained and washed chickpeas in a pan submerging them in water. Bring to a boil for 5 minutes, then cover and simmer on low for about 30 minutes. Drain and let cool.

Combine chickpeas with chopped onion, cumin, coriander, garlic, salt and chives in a mixing bowl. Mash chickpeas and combine all ingredients together very well. You may also use a food processor for this part. The key is creating a consistent texture. Then add flour to thicken and dry out the mixture.

Form the mixture into small balls, about 1 inch/2.5 cm in diameter and flatten slightly. The mixture should make about 8–10 balls. Heat oil to 375°F/190°C and gently drop the balls into the oil until dark golden brown. Remove and let excess oils drain on a strainer or paper towels. We want the balls to be crispy to create the right texture for the pizza assembly later.

(continued)

Combine all ingredients for hummus sauce in a food processor and blend until smooth. You'll notice that the consistency is slightly less thick than regular hummus to spread easier on the crust.

Combine all ingredients for veggie mix in bowl and toss together. Place in refrigerator until later.

If you're making two pies, remember to equally divide the ingredients between them for this part. Top the dough crust with shredded mozzarella and parbake for 5–7 minutes in preheated oven at 500°F/260°C. Remove pie but leave oven on. Spread a very light layer of hummus evenly across crust. Be careful not to add too much, or the pizza will get too heavy. Plus, you can save the leftover hummus and eat it with veggies. Break up falafel balls and evenly distribute. Bake for an additional 5 minutes. Slice and top with a scoop of veggie mix on each slice. Top with a dash of paprika for extra color.

POUTINE

We can thank the Quebecois for this delicious pie. A generous helping of hand-cut French fries meets melted cheese curds, topped off with a succulent gravy sauce. Possibly one of our all-time favorite street foods.

- -

ENOUGH DOUGH FOR 1 PIZZA (SEE P 19)

FRENCH FRIES

2 lb/907 g Yukon gold or russet potatoes

4 cups/950 mL oil for frying (vegetable or peanut works for us)

Salt and pepper

GRAVY

1½ cups/355 mL water

3 tsp/7 g beef bouillon

¼ cup/25 g flour

¼ cup/60 g butter

1 white onion, minced

½ tsp garlic

½ tsp black pepper

¼ cup/30 g shredded mozzarella
½ lb/230 g cheese curds

Wash cut potatoes in cold running water and soak for about an hour in cold water—although longer (up to 24 hours in the refrigerator) is ideal. Pat dry thoroughly.

Heat first batch of oil for fries to 325°F/163°C in a large pot or Dutch oven, with enough oil to submerge potatoes with several inches of space left before the top of the pot (potatoes will boil over otherwise). Cook potatoes for about 5 minutes in the oil and remove. Set on paper towel-lined plate to soak up excess oil. The potatoes will not be browned yet.

Turn the heat up to 400°F/204°C on the oil. Time to dip 'em in again for a second round of frying. This time keep the fries cooking in the oil until they're a nice golden brown. Remove and set on paper towel-lined plate. Sprinkle with salt and pepper. Set aside to cool for later.

Combine all ingredients for gravy in saucepan and bring to a boil, stirring frequently. Cook over medium heat until gravy thickens. Remove from heat and let cool.

Apply shredded mozzarella to dough evenly. Distribute French fries (go pretty heavy with these) to cover the cheese. Top with cheese curds and apply rings of gravy, starting at the outside and working toward the center. Bake in preheated oven at 500°F/260°C for 10–12 minutes until crust is golden brown.

GYRO

The quintessential street food, you can never go wrong with meat that comes from a giant spinning slab. Whatever you do, just don't call it a guy-ro. This recipe yields approximately two 12 inch/30.5 cm pizzas worth of ingredients.

- -

ENOUGH DOUGH FOR 2 PIZZAS (SEE P 19)

FRENCH FRIES

1 lb/455 g Yukon gold or russet potatoes

2 cups/475 mL oil for frying (vegetable or peanut works for us)

Salt and pepper

TZATZIKI SAUCE

1 cup/237 mL plain unflavored Greek yogurt

1 cucumber, seeded, peeled and chopped

1 tbsp/1 g fresh dill

½ tsp salt

2 tsp/5 g garlic powder

½ cup/60 g shredded mozzarella cheese

¾ cup/180 mL Simple Cream sauce (p 26)

½ lb/226 g gyro-style lamb meat, prepared (if you don't know how, see if you can pick some up from your local Greek restaurant or deli)

½ cup/80 g tomatoes, chopped

¼ cup/21 g white onion, sliced

½ cup/30 g shredded romaine lettuce

Wash cut potatoes in cold running water and soak for about 1 hour in cold water— although longer (up to 24 hour in the refrigerator) is ideal. Pat dry thoroughly.

Heat first batch of oil for fries to 325°F/163°C in a large pot or Dutch oven, with enough oil to submerge potatoes with several inches of space left before the top of the pot (potatoes will boil over otherwise). Cook potatoes for about 5 minutes in the oil and remove. Set on paper towel-lined plate to soak up excess oil. The potatoes will not be browned yet.

Turn the heat up to 400°F/204°C on the oil. Time to dip 'em in again for a second round of frying. This time keep the fries cooking in the oil until they're a nice golden brown. Remove and set on paper towel-lined plate. Sprinkle with salt and pepper. Set aside to cool for later.

Mix all ingredients for tzatziki sauce together until well blended. Refrigerate until ready to serve.

If you're making two pies, remember to split the ingredients equally between them for this part. Distribute mozzarella cheese on dough. Apply rings of Simple Cream sauce, starting at the outside closest to the crust and working toward the center. Distribute French fries then gyro meat. Bake in preheated oven at 500°F/260°C for 10–12 minutes until crust is golden brown. Slice pizza and top each slice with tomatoes, onions, lettuce and a drizzle of tzatziki sauce.

@ASHVINLAD CHICKEN CURRY

We've always been fans of crustomer pizza challenges. This one in particular has to be our favorite. Ashvin is a regular, both in store and on our Twitter feed. When he mentioned his disappointment that we had yet to make a Chicken Curry pie, we had to make it up to him. And not only that, but we even named the pie in his honor. Recipe yields three 12 inch/ 30.5 cm pizzas.

- -

ENOUGH DOUGH FOR 3 PIZZAS (SEE P 19)

GRILLED CHICKEN

3 skinless and boneless chicken breasts, cut in half
½ cup/118 mL blended oil
2 tbsp/15 g curry powder
½ tbsp/7 mL garlic, minced
½ tbsp/7 g ginger, minced
½ tbsp/5 g jalapeño, finely chopped

CURRY SAUCE

3 tbsp/28 g cornstarch
½ cup/120 mL cold water
1½ qt/1.5 L vegetable stock from bouillon cubes
½ cup/55 g curry powder
½ tbsp/8 mL garlic, minced
½ tbsp/7 g ginger, minced
½ tbsp/5 g jalapeño, finely chopped
Salt, to taste

VEGETABLES

1 cup/130 g carrots, peeled and chopped
½ cup/75 g white onion chopped
1 jalapeño, seeded and chopped
Salt and pepper
Oil for sautéing

¾ cup/90 g shredded mozzarella cheese

Marinate chicken in oil, curry, garlic, ginger and jalepeño for at least 1 hour (up to 24 hours chilled). Grill on medium heat until browned on the outside and cooked through. Let cool and slice into strips.

Combine cornstarch with cold water in a large pot. Add additional ingredients for curry sauce and bring to a boil. Add salt to taste. Lower heat and simmer for 10 minutes to thicken. Remove from heat and set aside.

Sauté all ingredients together for vegetable mix until the carrots soften and the onions are translucent. Combine with the grilled chicken strips.

If you're making all three pies, don't forget to split the ingredients equally during this part. Distribute shredded mozzarella. Apply rings of curry sauce, starting at the outside closest to the crust and working toward the center. Add chicken and vegetable mix. Drizzle a little more curry sauce on top. Bake in preheated oven at 500°F/260°C for 10–12 minutes. Slice and serve.

VINDALOO

In case you're not well versed in Indian cuisine, we'll save you the trouble of googling this. This dish is traditionally a curry dish made with pork and garlic from the region of Goa. Our version isn't necessarily traditional, but what else would you expect from us? Or haven't you learned anything from us yet? We do what we want. Recipe makes approximately two 12 inch/30.5 cm pizzas.

- -

ENOUGH DOUGH FOR 2 PIZZAS (SEE P 19)

2 tbsp/30 mL vegetable oil

1½ lb/680 g pork shoulder, sliced into 2"/5 cm cubes

Salt and pepper

3 medium onions diced

2 tbsp/12 g flour

2 tsp/4 g sweet paprika

½ tsp ground cumin

½ tsp ground cardamom

Dash of cayenne

Dash of cloves

1 cup/240 mL chicken stock (make it fresh, you lazy ass...uh can we say that?)

14.5 oz/397 g can diced tomatoes

1 tbsp/15 mL red wine vinegar

1 tsp mustard seeds

½ tsp sugar

1 bay leaf

¾ cup/90 g shredded mozzarella cheese

2 tbsp/2 g cilantro, minced

Add 1 tablespoon oil to a Dutch oven and heat to high. Salt and pepper pork as desired. Add pork (in batches if necessary, don't crowd 'em) and brown on all sides. Remove from pan and set aside.

Add the rest of the oil, the the onions and a pinch of salt. Reduce heat to medium and sauté (stirring frequently) until tender and translucent. Add flour, paprika, cumin, cardamom, cayenne and cloves. Cook until incorporated and fragrant, about 2 minutes, stirring constantly.

Slowly add chicken stock, stirring as you do. Add in half the can of tomatoes, vinegar, mustard seeds, sugar and bay leaf. Stir to incorporate everything, scraping up any browned bits from the bottom. Add pork and any accumulated juices and make sure meat is covered in the liquid. Add broth if necessary. Bring to a simmer, reduce heat to low and cook for 2 hours.

Using tongs, remove pork chunks. By this time they'll be very tender and may fall apart easily. Remove the bay leaf as well. Shred the pork and mix with the rest of the tomatoes. Using a stand or hand blender, blend sauce until smooth.

If you're making two pizzas, remember to split the ingredients equally for this part. Top dough with mozzarella. Add shredded pork and tomatoes on top. Drizzle sauce on top. Bake in preheated oven at 500°F/260°C for 10–12 minutes until crust is golden brown. Top off with cilantro. Slice and serve.

BRAZILIAN SHRIMP SOUP

Okay, so this is more of a stew than a soup, but it is going on a pizza so no need to get pizza technical about it. This pie features the mellow sweetness of coconut milk melding with okra, shrimp and a slight heat of red pepper flakes for the kicker. Recipe makes approximately two 12 inch/30.5 cm pizzas.

- -

ENOUGH DOUGH FOR 2 PIZZAS (SEE P 19)

1 tbsp/15 mL olive oil

½ white onion, chopped

½ green bell pepper, chopped

4–5 okra, sliced

1 tbsp/10 g fresh garlic, minced

1 cup/210 g rice

Dash of red pepper flakes

½ tsp salt

¾ cup/120 g canned diced tomatoes, drained

3 cups/710 mL water

½ cup/120 mL coconut milk

Dash of black pepper

½ tbsp/8 mL lemon juice

¼ cup/4 g cilantro

1¼ lb/570 g small shrimp, peeled and tails removed

¾ cup/90 g shredded mozzarella

Fresh cilantro, chopped for topping

Heat oil in large pot and add onions, bell pepper, okra and garlic until vegetables soften. Add rice and stir until rice is coated in oil. Add the red pepper flakes, salt, tomatoes, water, coconut milk, black pepper and lemon juice and stir. Stir consistently until the rice is cooked and the sauce thickens. Once rice is cooked, turn heat to low and add the cilantro and shrimp. Stir until shrimp turns pink. Remove from heat and let thicken while cooling.

If you're making two pies, remember to split the ingredients equally between the two for this part. Using a spatula, gently apply a thick layer of soup mix to the dough. Make sure shrimp are evenly dispersed across the dough. Top with shredded mozzarella. Bake in preheated oven at 500°F/260°C for 10–12 minutes until crust is golden brown. Top with fresh cilantro. Slice and serve.

6

CHICAGO STAPLES

There are a few culinary rites of passage that you must complete upon moving to the Windy City in order to be considered a "real Chicagoan" (said in an old-school Chicago accent, probably by a dude with a mustache wearing a Bears jersey). These meals often involve lots of cheese, meat and bread. And to prove our true Chicagoan-ness, we once spent a whole month re-creating some of our favorite landmark Chicago meals as pizzas. Sure, we gained a few pounds, but it was well worth it for the many varieties of sausages we enjoyed (seriously, Chicagoans love 'em some sausage).

Whether you're a born and raised Chicagoan or have never visited the Second City, these pizzas will engulf your taste buds in mustard-covered, au jus-drizzled and powder sugar-coated happiness. Among the classics, we've also included a few 'za creations inspired by our favorite Chicago neighborhoods and people (hint: we're talking about world champion wrestler CM Punk here, people!). And just so it's out in the open, the answer is "No, we did not include a deep dish pizza recipe." It's just not our style.

Besides, we're sure there are far more flavorful, interesting and memorable meals that this city can offer you. Are you ready to see just what we're talkin' about? Go ahead! Turn the page. The *real* Taste of Chicago awaits you.

CM PUNK'S ANACONDA VICE

When we got the chance to make not one, but two pizzas for wrestling megastar and Chicago native CM Punk, we knew they should take inspiration from our favorite of Punk's finishing moves. Thus, we present to you the headlock of flavor, the knock-you-out with deliciousness: Anaconda Vice.

- -

ENOUGH DOUGH FOR 1 PIZZA (SEE P 19)

1½ cup/360 g black beans, cooked with 2 tsp/5 g bacon bits mixed in

1½ cup/165 g ground fully cooked or Upton's chorizo sausage seitan

½ cup/80 g tomatoes, chopped

½ cup/50 g green onions, chopped

3 tbsp/ 3 g fresh parsley, finely chopped

3 tbsp/3 g fresh cilantro, finely chopped

Apply black bean and bacon bit mixture gently onto dough using a spatula. Distribute chorizo. Bake in preheated oven at 500°F/260°C for 10–12 minutes until crust is golden brown. Top with tomatoes, onions, parsley and cilantro. Slice and serve.

PACZKI PIZZA

Fat Tuesday means one very wonderfully sweet and sugary thing for Chicagoans: Paczki Day— a day of filling your piehole with as many of these mini Polish doughnuts as you can get your hands on (and grab quickly, because they sell out fast). The demand was so high, in fact, that we decided to make our own version.

- -

ENOUGH DOUGH FOR 2 PIZZAS (THE EXTRA IS FOR THE TOPPER) (SEE P19)

SWEET CHEESE FILLING

½ cup/115 g cottage cheese or ricotta

1 tbsp/30 g cream cheese

1 egg yolk

1 tbsp/12 g sugar

1 tsp vanilla

1 tsp lemon juice

Dash of salt

FRUIT MIXTURE

1 pt/300 g raspberries

½ cup/95 g sugar

¼ cup/60 mL water

1 tbsp/9 g cornstarch

1 tsp lemon juice

¾ cup/90 g shredded mozzarella

Confectioners' sugar

Blend all ingredients for sweet cheese filling in food processor until smooth.

Heat raspberries and sugar in saucepan. Mix water and cornstarch until fully combined. Slowly stir in cornstarch mixture. Add lemon juice and continue to stir. Cook on medium heat until sauce is thickened. Remove from heat and let cool.

Using a spatula, gently apply sweet cheese filling to dough. Distribute shredded mozzarella. Drizzle raspberry sauce over cheese. Stretch extra dough thinly without any crust and spread over the pie. Cut 4–5 holes in the crust to prevent it from bubbling up. Bake in preheated oven at 500°F/260°C for 10–12 minutes until crust and topper are golden brown. Top with powdered sugar. Serve hot or let cool and serve at room temperature.

THE ARGYLE

In Chicago, the Argyle red line stop on the CTA "L" train system is a go-to spot for authentic Vietnamese cuisine. Inspired by flavors from this 'hood, the Argyle pizza brings in a fusion of Asian flavors, including spicy Sriracha sauce, peanut satay, tofu and traditional toppers such as bean sprouts and cilantro. It also just so happens to be vegan. Recipe yields approximately three 12 inch/30.5 cm pizzas

- -

ENOUGH DOUGH FOR 3 PIZZAS (SEE P 19)

TOFU

16 oz/455 g firm tofu, pressed and cubed

1 tbsp/15 mL soy sauce

1 tbsp/15 mL hot sauce, we suggest Sriracha sauce

1 tbsp/15 mL sesame oil

PEANUT SATAY

¼ cup/60 mL coconut milk

3 tbsp/45 mL hot sauce, we suggest Sriracha

¾ cup/135 g peanut butter (if you're preparing this vegan, make sure your peanut butter is labeled vegan)

1 tbsp/15 mL soy sauce

1 tbsp/15 mL sesame oil

4 cloves fresh garlic, crushed or minced

3 tbsp/8 g thinly sliced lemongrass

⅓ cup/80 mL oil

1 medium yellow onion, sliced thin

1 head of garlic, peeled and crushed

Hand full of fresh cilantro, stems removed and chopped

2 cups/180 g fresh bean sprouts

Toss all ingredients for tofu together and allow the mixture to marinate for 20 minutes.

Place all ingredients for the peanut satay in a small heavy-bottomed saucepan and simmer over medium to low heat for 5 minutes or until the sauce is smooth. Let cool and set aside until you are ready to assemble the pizza.

Fry lemongrass in oil over medium heat for 5 minutes until brown. If you are using the fibrous green tops, then strain lemongrass out of the flavored oil (note: if you have access to a specialty food store that can provide lemongrass with only the tender white bottoms, then there is no need to strain them out). Add onion to the oil and fry until golden. Remove from heat and add chopped garlic. Stir gently until the oil stops bubbling and the garlic has taken on a light brown color. Drain the onion and garlic mix.

If you're making three pizzas, remember to split the ingredients equally among them for this part. Apply rings of satay sauce onto dough, starting from the outside ring closest to the crust and working toward the center. Distribute the marinated tofu in a thin layer to cover the dough completely. Add lemongrass and fried onion and garlic mix across the tofu. Bake in preheated oven at 500°F/260°C for 10–12 minutes until crust is golden brown. Let cool for 5 minutes. Top with cilantro and bean sprouts to your liking. Optional: add rings of Sriracha sauce for an extra spicy kick.

CHI-STYLE HOT DOG

The original ballpark dog, with all the fixings. You better keep that ketchup far, far away from this pie! Mustaches, baseball hats and old-school Chicago accents are always welcome though.

- -

ENOUGH DOUGH FOR 1 PIZZA (SEE P 19)

¾ cup/180 mL Simple Cream sauce (p 26)

½ cup/60 g mozzarella cheese, shredded

1 cup/240 g hot dogs, sliced

3 tbsp/50 g relish (Chicago-style neon green)

¼ cup/21 g white onion, chopped

¼ cup/40 g tomatoes, chopped

¼ cup/40 g sport peppers, chopped

2 tbsp/30 g celery salt

3 tbsp/25 g poppy seeds

Yellow mustard

Sliced dill pickle spears (optional)

Apply the Simple Cream sauce in rings starting at the outside closest to the crust, and work toward the center. Distribute shredded mozzarella, hot dog slices, relish, onions, tomatoes, sport peppers, in that order, evenly across the pie. Bake in preheated oven at 500°F/260°C for 10–12 minutes until crust is golden brown. Top with rings of yellow mustard, and a sprinkle of celery salt and poppy seeds. Slice and serve. Optional: add a sliced dill pickle spear on top of each slice.

18TH STREET

This pie is an ode to one of our favorite streets in the city to find traditional Mexican cusine. Featuring nopales (aka cactus) you may even get a few hallucinations after too many slices of this spicy, filling pizza.

- -

ENOUGH DOUGH FOR 1 PIZZA (SEE P 19)

PICO DE GALLO

1 cup/160 g tomatoes, finely chopped

½ cup/45 g red onion, finely chopped

2 tbsp/20 g jalapeños, seeded and finely chopped

2 tbsp/2 g fresh cilantro, finely chopped

3 tbsp/45 mL lemon juice

1 tsp salt

ENCHILADA SAUCE

3 tbsp/45 mL olive oil

3 tbsp/19 g flour

¼ cup/30 g chili powder

2 cups/475 mL chicken broth

1 tsp cumin

2 tsp/5 g garlic powder

¾ tsp salt

½ tsp sugar

1 cup/230 g cooked black beans

1 small jar nopales, drained and sliced

¾ cup/90 g cheddar cheese

1 ripe avocado

Combine ingredients for pico de gallo in mixing bowl and refrigerate. For optimum flavor, prepare this the day before and allow it to chill overnight. Otherwise, give it an hour or so to sit.

Heat oil for enchilada sauce in a small pan. When oil is hot, add the flour and cook for a few more minutes, stirring with a wire whisk. Add chili powder and stir until mixed. Slowly add chicken broth, stirring constantly. Add cumin, garlic powder, salt and sugar. Continue to stir as you bring it to a boil. Boil for 3 to 5 minutes. Remove from heat and let cool.

Apply cooked black beans over dough gently using a spatula. Distribute nopales evenly. Bake in preheated oven at 500°F/260°C for 8–10 minutes. Remove pizza, but leave the oven on. Top with pico de gallo and cheddar cheese. Add rings of enchilada sauce, starting at the outside closest to the crust and moving toward the center. Bake for an additional 5 minutes. Slice avocado into small pieces evenly onto the pizza. Slice and serve.

MILWAUKEE AVE.

There are many Chicago traditions we can thank the Poles for, and eating kielbasa is definitely toward the top of our list. Polish culture has historically been a huge part of Chicago's heritage, and that includes influences on food. Paczki, pierogi, pickles, oh my! Here's our take on some of our favorite Polish foods turned into a pizza.

- -

ENOUGH DOUGH FOR 1 PIZZA (SEE P 19)

1 white onion, sliced thin

2 tsp/10 mL olive oil

½ cup/120 mL water

¾ cup/180 mL Simple Cream sauce (p 26)

1 lb/455 g kielbasa sausage, grilled and sliced

½ cup/60 g mozzarella cheese, shredded

Brown mustard

About ½ cup/60 g Polish dill pickles, sliced

Add white onion and olive oil in pan on medium heat. Stir in water and bring to boil. Cook until water is fully evaporated and onions turn a deep brown color. Remove from heat and set aside.

Apply the Simple Cream sauce in rings, starting at the outside closest to the crust and working toward the center. Distribute mozzarella, then kielbasa and onions. Bake in preheated oven at 500°F/260°C for 10–12 minutes until crust is golden brown. Top with rings of brown mustard and sliced pickles. Slice and serve.

THE REUBEN

You're not a true Chicagoan until you've survived a St. Paddy's Day weekend. Festivities start in the wee early hours with green beer and a green river to match. Then begins a daylong celebration of all things "Chi-rish." This pie keeps the party going strong through the night.

ENOUGH DOUGH FOR 1 PIZZA (SEE P 19)

¼ cup/30 g shredded mozzarella

RUSSIAN DRESSING

½ cup/110 mL mayo

2 tbsp/30 mL ketchup

2 tbsp/30 mL relish

½ tbsp/8 mL white vinegar

¼ tsp Worcestershire sauce

¼ tsp salt

¼ tsp celery salt

1 lb/455 g shredded corned beef

½ cup/70 g sauerkraut

¾ cup/90 g shredded Swiss cheese

Distribute shredded mozzarella across dough and add Russian dressing over it in rings, starting at the outside closest to the crust and working toward the center. Top with corned beef. Bake in preheated oven at 500°F/260°C for 10–12 minutes until golden brown. Immediately out of the oven, top with sauerkraut and Swiss cheese. Let cheese melt. You can always put it back in the oven (turned off but still warm) to speed up this process. Slice and serve.

TAYLOR STREET

If you want authentic Italian food in Chicago, look no farther than Taylor Street. Though we're always tempted to imagine scenes from gang movies when we're here, it's really just good food and good people that you'll find. And as you already know, we can't deny an opportunity to put noodles on pizza.

- -

ENOUGH DOUGH FOR 1 PIZZA (SEE P 19)

WHITE CLAM SAUCE

2 tbsp/30 mL roux (olive oil and flour)

6.5 oz/185 g can of clam meat with juice

16 oz/455 g can chopped tomatoes with juice

1 tbsp/1 g fresh parsley, finely chopped

1 tsp garlic powder

1 tbsp/15 mL white dry cooking wine

Juice of 1 lemon

¼ tsp red chili flakes

¼ tsp black pepper

1 cup/140 g cooked shell pasta

¾ cup/90 g shredded mozzarella

⅓ cup/60 g Parmesan, grated

1 tbsp/1 g fresh parsley, finely chopped

In a large sauté pan, make olive oil and flour roux, then add the remainder of the ingredients for sauce. Cook over medium heat until the sauce boils. Simmer for 10 minutes to thicken over low heat.

Mix sauce and shells together.

Apply shredded mozzarella to dough evenly. Spread shell and sauce mixture gently over cheese. Bake in preheated oven at 500°F /60°C for 10–12 minutes until crust is golden brown. Top with Parmesan and parsley. Optional: add a drizzle of olive oil and red pepper flakes. Slice and serve.

ITALIAN BEEF

The Italian beef (which can't be eaten without giardiniera, in our book) is a staple of late-night, quick service food spots in Chicago. Double-dipped in au jus and dripping (literally) with meaty goodness, what's not to love?

ENOUGH DOUGH FOR 1 PIZZA (SEE P 19)

BEEF

3 lb/1,361 g beef brisket

16 oz/475 mL can beef consommé

1 cup/240 mL of water

3 tbsp/45 mL soy sauce

2 cloves garlic, chopped

1 cup/240 mL marinara sauce (p 27)

¾ cup/90 g shredded mozzarella

¾ cup/180 g mild giardiniera, drained

Combine ingredients for brisket in a roasting pan and marinate overnight in the refrigerator. Cover with aluminum foil and bake in preheated oven at 300°F/149°C for about 3 hours, or until meat is tender and breaks apart with fork. Let cool and shred beef. Save that beef juice!

Apply marinara sauce to dough (see tips on p 28). Top with most of shredded mozzarella. Distribute shredded beef, followed by mild giardiniera. Add remaining mozzarella. Drizzle a little of the juice left in the pan from the beef over the pie. Bake in preheated oven at 500°F/260°C for 10–12 minutes until crust is golden brown and cheese is melted. Slice and serve.

SLICES
AND
SALAD

THIS A WAY

BREAKING
THE RULES
TASTES
PRETTY
GOOD.

1615

zaa precycle

BREW
S & PINTS
THE SLICE
PIES
E-TO-ORDER SALADS
O-BROWNIES
Y THE BOTTLE

DESCHUTES

7

COMIDA CALIENTE

We're just going to go out on a limb here and admit something to you. Spicy 'za is our favorite. We offer red pepper flakes, a spicy ranch and two types of hot sauce free at our restaurants for a reason. And that reason is a selfish one. We eat our own pizzas with these wonderfully fiery toppers. Oh, we can't forget our tomatillo salsa (p 133), which we would probably take shots of if offered the opportunity. Somebody dare us, please!

The following recipes are spins on our favorite Mexican fare, with an added picante kick. Tacos, burritos and quesadillas are all easily transformed into pizzas by replacing tortillas with pizza dough. But we've also included on the list our all-time favorite Mexican street food: elotes. There's also a collaboration we did with the grilling masters at ManBQue on a mole sauce with pork belly that will knock you out (if you're a fan of meat, beer and rock 'n' roll, you should check out ManBQue, too!).

Truthfully, most of these pizzas are all about the sauce. If you want specifics, we're talking about enchilada sauce, avocado tomatillo salsa, Sriracha lime sauce, puya pepper salsa and mole sauce, to name a few. And if you take spicy as seriously as we do, always remember to make a little extra for dipping.

ELOTES

This is a summer street food staple. We've taken this popular grilled and slathered snack and transferred it from the cob to a crust. Either way, it's quick and easy—both to make and to eat. Watch this pie disappear in front of a hungry group of friends in record time.

- -

ENOUGH DOUGH FOR 1 PIZZA (SEE P 19)

4–5 ears sweet corn in husks

CILANTRO LIME SAUCE

½ cup/60 mL Mexican cream (or sour cream)

2 tbsp/30 mL lime juice

1 bunch cilantro

1 tsp chili salt

¼ cup/30 g shredded mozzarella cheese

3 tbsp/45 mL melted butter

¾ cup/90 g cotija cheese

Chili salt

Grill corn on the cob in husks until they blister, about 10–15 minutes. Let cool and cut corn off the cob.

Mix together ingredients for cilantro lime sauce.

Add shredded mozzarella and apply rings of cilantro lime sauce, starting at the outside closest to the crust and working toward the center. Distribute grilled corn. Bake in preheated oven at 500°F/260°C for 10–12 minutes until crust is golden brown. Top with a drizzle of melted butter, cotija cheese and a sprinkle of chili salt. Add more cilantro lime sauce as desired. Slice and serve.

EST CHEC
Guests
Server
/SAL – ENTREE – VEG/POT – D
Thank You - P ase Com
GFS REORDER NO. 279544

SPINACH AND BEAN QUESADILLA

The versatile spinach and fava bean purée makes for a zesty base, made even more irresistible when combined with ground chorizo and tomatillo salsa. We recommend using this base to experiment with a variety of your favorite veggies and meat combos. This recipe yields approximately two 12 inch/30.5 cm pizzas.

- -

ENOUGH DOUGH FOR 4 PIZZAS (EACH PIE REQUIRES AN ADDITIONAL DOUGH FOR TOPPING) (SEE P 19)

TOMATILLO SALSA

2 large jalapeños

10 tomatillos

¼ bunch cilantro

¾ tsp fresh garlic, minced

½ tbsp/8 g salt

SPINACH AND BEAN MIX

1½ cups/60 g sautéed spinach (recipe on p 40)

1 can fava beans, cooked

½ tsp fresh garlic, crushed

½ tsp cumin

½ tsp chili powder

Salt and pepper to taste

1 lb/455 g ground chorizo, cooked

¾ cup/90 g shredded cheddar cheese

¼ cup/4 g fresh cilantro, stems removed and chopped

Bring a large pot of water to a boil. Cut stems off jalapeños and add to boiling water. Remove husks and stems from tomatillos. When peppers turn a dark green color, add tomatillos. Boil for several minutes until tomatillos lose their bright green color and are soft. Using a spoon to keep jalapeños and tomatillos in the pot, pour water from pot into sink, leaving a little bit of water in the pot (just enough to cover tomatillos and peppers). Put pot in refrigerator. When the tomatillos and peppers have cooled, use a slotted spoon to move them into a food processor. Add cilantro, garlic and salt. Purée for about 1 minute until salsa is smooth.

Blend spinach and beans together in the blender. Mix in garlic, cumin and chili powder. Add salt and pepper to taste.

If you're making two pies, remember to split the ingredients equally between them for this part. Apply spinach and bean mixture to dough using a spatula. Add chorizo and top with shredded cheddar and fresh cilantro. Stretch second layer of dough thinly enough (and without a crust) to appear translucent when held to the light. Add second layer to each pie and poke several holes in the dough to keep it from bubbling up during baking. Bake in preheated oven at 500°F/260°C for 10–12 minutes until crust is golden brown. Top with tomatillo salsa. Slice and serve.

ANA'S RAJAS CON CREMA

When our prep team shares a new pizza concept, we listen. This pie comes courtesy of Ana, one of our very talented prep cooks. The dish is simple, but rich in flavor. It's also very versatile and goes well with grilled or battered chicken added on top of the pie.

- -

ENOUGH DOUGH FOR 1 PIZZA (SEE P 19)

5–7 poblano peppers
1 white onion, sliced
Olive oil
1 tsp salt
1 tbsp/15 mL chicken bouillon
½ cup/110 g sweet corn
1 cup/240 mL Simple Cream (p 26)
2 small tortilla shells
Grilled chicken (optional)
1 cup/120 g shredded mozzarella

Grill the whole poblano peppers until the outsides are charred. Let cool then slice the peppers into small strips.

In a pan, cook sliced onions with oil until softened. Add sliced poblano peppers and salt. Stir until combined and add chicken bouillon and sweet corn. Stir in Simple Cream sauce and simmer on low for about 15 minutes. Set aside to cool.

Slice tortilla shells into small strips. Cook in a hot pan with a very small amount of oil until browned. Set aside.

You may also want to add grilled chicken on top of mixture on your pizza. See our recipe for grilled chicken strips on p 135.

Apply most of the mozzarella onto the dough. Spread poblano mixture onto the pizza dough. Drizzle any leftover sauce on top of mixture. Top with remaining mozzarella. Optional: add grilled chicken. Bake in preheated oven at 500°F/260°C for 10–12 minutes until crust is golden brown. Top with tortilla strips. Slice and serve.

CHILAQUILES

Step aside "brunch," there's a new reason to eat eggs after 11 a.m. Essentially, chilaquiles are a wonderful combination of scrambled eggs with nachos. Genius. And they beat an omelet or overpriced breakfast burrito any day. Recipe yields approximately two 12 inch/30.5 cm pizzas.

- -

ENOUGH DOUGH FOR 2 PIZZAS (SEE P 19)

GRILLED CHICKEN

2 chicken breasts

¾ cup/180 mL white vinegar

1 cup/240 mL olive oil

½ cup/20 g fresh basil, chopped finely

½ tbsp/8 g salt

½ tbsp/5 g fresh garlic

¼ cup/10 g fresh parsley, chopped finely

PUYA SALSA

2 large Roma tomatoes

10 dried puya chilies

½ tbsp/5 g fresh garlic, minced

½ tbsp/8 g salt

½ cup/120 mL water

1 cup/240 mL sour cream

3 tbsp/45 mL buttermilk

SCRAMBLED EGGS

5–6 eggs

1 tsp whole milk

Salt and pepper

½ cup/60 g shredded mozzarella cheese

Corn chips (about 2 handfuls)

½ cup/60 g shredded cheddar cheese

1 avocado

Place all the ingredients for the chicken breasts in a large pan. Use your hands to evenly coat the chicken breast with the ingredients. Cover and place in refrigerator overnight.

Preheat grill or nonstick pan on a medium-high temperature. When grill is hot, lay chicken breasts flat on the grill. Flip the chicken and cook the other side until chicken is cooked through. Let chicken cool. Cut into small strips.

Grill the Roma tomatoes until they are cooked and the skins are slightly charred. Remove from heat and let cool. In a skillet, toast chilies for several minutes. Remove from heat and let cool. Wearing latex gloves to protect your hands, remove stems and seeds from chilies. Add tomatoes and chilies to the food processor along with the garlic and salt. Blend for several minutes until smooth. Add water a little bit at a time until desired consistency is reached.

Cut sour cream with buttermilk and set aside until you are ready to assemble the pizza.

Whisk together eggs, milk, salt and pepper. Scramble in a nonstick pan for several minutes, leaving the eggs formed but not quite fully cooked through (they will finish cooking in the oven).

If you're making two pizzas, remember to equally divide the ingredients for this part. Distribute mozzarella cheese over dough. Apply rings of sour cream, starting at the outside closest to the crust and moving toward the center. Add egg mixture evenly over sauce, followed by grilled chicken. Bake in preheated oven at 500°F/260°C for 8–10 minutes. Remove pizza but leave oven on. Break up corn chips over hot pizza. Top with cheddar cheese. Bake for an additional 5 minutes until cheese melts and crust is golden brown. Cut avocado into slices and distribute over pizza. Top with puya salsa. Slice and serve.

FISH TACO

It's not officially summer until you've had your fair share of fish tacos. This recipe is an Asian fusion take on traditional fish tacos with fresh cabbage slaw and Sriracha cilantro sauce, brought together with fried catfish bites. For this one, you can cut your dough into two smaller pies to mimic taco shells and create individual pizza servings.

- -

ENOUGH DOUGH FOR 1 PIZZA (SEE P 19)

SLAW

1 cup/340 g red cabbage, shredded

1 tbsp/15 mL olive oil

1 tsp lime juice

1 tsp hot sauce, we recommend Sriracha

3 tbsp/3 g fresh cilantro, chopped

¼ cup/21 g white onion, finely chopped

Dash of salt and pepper

FRIED CATFISH BATTER

4 cups/400 g flour

4 tbsp/25 g season salt

2 eggs

1 cup/240 mL heavy cream

3 skinless and boneless catfish fillets, cut into strips

4 cups/950 mL frying oil (amount may vary depending on size of pan)

1 cup/100 g flour

1 tsp salt

1 tsp black pepper

SAUCE

2 cups/275 g sour cream

2 tbsp/30 mL lime juice

1 tbsp/15 mL Sriracha

¼ cup/4 g fresh cilantro, chopped

1 tsp fresh garlic, minced

¾ cup/90 g shredded mozzarella

½ cup/115 g queso fresco

¼ cup/4 g fresh cilantro, chopped

Combine ingredients for slaw, mix well and set in refrigerator for about 1 hour (up to 24 hours) to marinate.

Mix all ingredients together for fish batter. Dip catfish strips into batter and set aside for 10 minutes. Preheat oil to 375°F/190°C in a large pot, with enough oil to submerge fish strips. Dip battered strips in flour mixed with salt and pepper then place into hot oil. Cook until crispy and golden brown. Let cool and cut into small chunks.

Mix ingredients together for sauce in a blender or food processor until well blended. Set aside until you are ready to assemble the pizza.

Distribute shredded mozzarella. Apply rings of sauce onto dough, starting at the outside closest to the crust and working toward the center. Distribute fish pieces. Bake in preheated oven at 500°F/260°C for 10–12 minutes until crust is golden brown. Top with queso fresco, slaw and cilantro. Slice and serve.

CHICKEN ENCHILADA QUESADILLA

Spicy chicken meets rich enchilada sauce, all held together by a quesadilla crust topper. Careful. This slice may seem simple, but it packs a punch of heat. This recipe yields approximately two 12 inch/30.5 cm pizzas.

- -

ENOUGH DOUGH FOR 4 PIZZAS (YOU'LL NEED TWO FOR TOPPERS) (SEE P 19)

ENCHILADA SAUCE

3 tbsp/45 mL blended oil

3 tbsp/21 g flour

¼ cup/30 g chili powder

2 cups/475 mL chicken broth (can use chicken base and water)

1 tsp cumin

2 tsp/5 g garlic powder

¾ tsp salt

½ tsp sugar

SPICY CHICKEN

2 skinless, boneless chicken breast, cubed

1¼ tsp/ 6 g salt

1¼ cup/300 mL hot sauce, we suggest Frank's Red Hot Sauce

1½ tbsp/13 g Cayenne pepper

½ cup/60 g shredded mozzarella cheese

½ cup/60 g shredded cheddar cheese

Cracked black pepper

For enchilada sauce, heat oil in a small pan. When oil is hot, add the flour and cook for a few minutes, stirring with a wire whisk. Add chili powder and stir until mixed. Slowly add chicken broth, stirring constantly. Add cumin, garlic powder, salt and sugar. Continue to stir as you bring to a boil. Boil for 3–5 minutes. Remove from heat and let cool. Set aside until you are ready to assemble the pizza.

Add chicken and salt for spicy chicken recipe to a large pan. Cook on medium heat, moving the chicken about occasionally until it's cooked through. Remove from heat and drain in colander. Rinse out pan. When chicken has drained, return to pan and place in refrigerator to cool. Once the chicken has cooled, add hot sauce and cayenne pepper to pan and mix well with gloved hands.

If you're making two pies, remember to split the ingredients equally during this part. Distribute shredded mozzarella to dough, followed by an even layer of spicy chicken. Top with cheddar, saving a small amount. Stretch extra dough out without a crust until it looks translucent when held to the light. Apply over pizza and poke several holes in the dough to keep it from bubbling up during baking. Bake in preheated oven at 500°F/260°C for 10–12 minutes until crust is golden brown. Top with remaining cheddar, enchilada sauce and cracked black pepper. Allow cheese to melt. Slice and serve.

GUACAMOLE BURRITO

This is a staple on our summer menu. A hearty rice and bean base combines with authentic flavors of freshly made guacamole and melted cheddar cheese. It's a heavy slice, so make sure you watch the proportions of each ingredient you add, ensuring it doesn't become overstuffed. Recipe yields approximately three 12 inch/30.5 cm pizzas.

- -

ENOUGH DOUGH FOR 3 PIZZAS (SEE P 19)

3 cups/660 g black beans
2½ cups/590 mL water
1 tsp fresh garlic, minced
1 tbsp/15 g salt
½ white onion, sliced
½ cup/120 mL blended oil

1 cup/210 g white rice
½ tsp fresh garlic
1½ tsp/8 g salt
¼ cup/45 g green pepper, diced
¼ cup/45 g red pepper, diced
¼ cup/21 g onion, diced
1¼ cups/295 mL water

GUACAMOLE

8 avocados, skin and pits removed
2 tomatoes, finely chopped
1 red onion, finely chopped
3 jalapeños, seeded
and finely chopped
1 tbsp/15 g salt or to taste
½ cup/8 g fresh cilantro,
finely chopped

½ cup/120 mL sour cream
1 tbsp/15 mL heavy cream
1 cup/120 g shredded cheddar cheese

Submerge black beans in water in a large pan with garlic and salt. Cook on medium heat until beans are soft and water evaporates.

Cook sliced onion in blended oil until onion is browned. Remove onion and pour oil over beans. Set aside for later.

Combine rice with garlic, salt, peppers and onion in water. Bring to a boil, then lower heat. Cover and simmer until water evaporates. Combine rice mixture with beans.

Combine all ingredients for guacamole in blender and mix together.

Cut sour cream with heavy cream and mix until blended. Set aside until you are ready to assemble the pizza.

Using a spatula, gently apply a light topping of rice and beans mixture to the dough. Parbake in preheated oven at 500°F/260°C for 8 minutes. Remove pizza and allow to cool for at least 10 minutes. Apply a light layer of guacamole on top of the rice and beans mixture using a spatula. Top with shredded cheddar. Bake for an additional 5–7 minutes until the crust is golden brown.

Finish with rings of sour cream, starting at the outside closest to the crust and working toward the center. Slice and serve.

UNHOLY MOLE!

We created this pizza in collaboration with our friends from ManBQue, a Chicago-based grilling, music and beer lifestyle organization. It all started with a launch party for the Unholy Mole Stout, a chipotle-flavored stout that ManBQue brewed with the Chicago-based Lake Effect Brewing Company. The distinctive heat of this beer required an equally distinctive pizza. Working closely with meat master and ManBQue creator, Jesse Valenciana, we created this delicious mole pizza that packs one helluva fiery punch. Warning: this ingredient list is fairly complex. Recipe yields approximately two 12 inch/30.5 cm pizzas.

- -

ENOUGH DOUGH FOR 2 PIZZAS (SEE P 19)

PICO DE GALLO

1 cup/160 g tomatoes, finely chopped

½ cup/43 g red onion, finely chopped

2 tbsp/20 g jalapeños, seeded and finely chopped

2 tbsp/2 g fresh cilantro, finely chopped

3 tbsp/45 mL lemon juice

1 tsp salt

TOMATILLO SALSA

2 large jalapeños

10 tomatillos

¼ bunch cilantro

¼ tbsp fresh garlic, minced

½ tbsp/8 g salt

MOLE

2 dried pasilla chiles

2 dried mulato chiles

1 dried ancho chile

1 guajillo chile

½ yellow onion, sliced

6 cloves garlic

3 cups/710 mL water

2 tbsp/30 mL grape seed oil

1 cup/237 mL dark coffee, brewed

1 cup/237 mL natural ketchup

¼ cup/50 g turbinado sugar (brown sugar works as well)

1 tbsp/15 g kosher salt

1 tbsp/3 g Mexican oregano

1 tbsp/7 g cumin

1 tbsp/5 g ground clove

4 tbsp/60 mL apple cider vinegar

2 tbsp/14 g unsweetened cocoa

1 tbsp/ 8 g cinnamon

½ tbsp/7 mL blue agave

1 cup/237 mL chicken broth

8 chicken thighs

Olive oil (approximately 2 tbsp {30 mL} for coating chicken)

Salt and pepper to taste

½ cup/60 g shredded mozzarella

½ cup/115 g queso fresco

(continued)

Combine ingredients for pico de gallo in mixing bowl and refrigerate. For optimum flavor, prepare this the day before and allow it to chill overnight. Otherwise, give it 1 hour or so to sit.

Bring a large pot of water to a boil. Cut stems off of jalapeños and add to boiling water. Remove husks and stems from tomatillos. When peppers turn a dark green color, add tomatillos. Boil for several minutes until tomatillos lose their bright green color and are soft. Using a spoon to keep jalapeños and tomatillos in the pot, pour water from pot into sink, leaving a little bit of water in the pot (just enough to cover tomatillos). Put pot in refrigerator. When the tomatillos and peppers have cooled, use a slotted spoon to move them into a food processor. Add cilantro, garlic and salt. Purée for about a minute until salsa is smooth. Refrigerate until you're ready to assemble the pizza.

Next is the mole. On a griddle, toast the chilies, yellow onions and garlic until dark and fragrant. The onions and garlic should be brown on both sides. This should only take about 3–4 minutes per side. While they are cooking, boil approximately 3 cups/710 mL of water separately.

Once browned, set the onions and garlic aside to cool. When the chilies are toasted, place them in a medium bowl and add the boiling water to rehydrate for about 15 minutes.

Drain the chilies, reserving the soaking water. Remove seeds from the chilies, and then purée the chilies, onion and garlic in a blender with enough of the soaking water to make a smooth paste.

In a heavy Dutch oven, heat the grape seed oil over medium heat, add the chili purée and coffee. Cook for about 5 minutes, stirring often.

Combine all the remaining ingredients for the mole except the chicken broth and cook over medium heat for about 15 minutes, stirring often.

Stir in the chicken broth and cook over low heat for an additional 45 minutes. Put aside to cool.

Preheat your oven's broiler and adjust the rack to be approximately 6–8 inches/15–20 cm from the heat source. Coat chicken thighs in olive oil and add salt and pepper to taste. Place chicken thighs skin side down on the broiler pan and broil for 10 minutes. Turn thighs over and broil for an additional 10–12 minutes until the chicken reaches an internal temperature of 165°F/74°C. Let cool and then shred off the bone. Mix a little less than half of the mole sauce with the shredded chicken and set aside.

If you're making two pies, remember to split the ingredients equally between them for this part. Place mozzarella on top of the stretched dough. Apply mole sauce in rings, starting from the outside and moving toward the center. Add shredded chicken. Bake in preheated oven at 500°F/260°C for 10 minutes. Remove pizza and add queso fresco and pico de gallo. Apply the tomatillo salsa in rings, starting from the outside and working toward the center. Slice and serve.

ACKNOWLEDGMENTS

It's important to acknowledge the hard work and effort put in by everyone to help this book come to fruition. Business is best done by teams of people. I first heard that from the late Steve Jobs and it has stuck with me and been continually reinforced time and time again. Without the team, we are nothing. With them, we can move mountains. Here are just a few of the people who helped us get to the finish line.

Thanks to Fredy for his patience and unrelenting hard work; Chris, for his calming demeanor and knack for reminding us to enjoy what we do; Brandon Price for his ability to take action and add in a little humor at just the right time; and Celia Marks for her creativity and pizza concept ingenuity. But most of all, I must acknowledge Ann Wanserski. Without her none of this would have been possible. She worked as one-part pizza stylist, one-part word weaver, and one-part badass to help preserve Dimo's unconventional spirit. She is one of a kind and I wouldn't trade her friendship for anything in the world.

I'd also like to thank my photographer, Ted Axelrod, who couldn't have been a better match for me; my publisher, Will Kiester, and his Page Street team who kept us on track and made sure we didn't miss a single deadline (even when we did); the copy editor Sarah, who caught all the little details; and the courageous and honest recipe testers, who kept us on our toes and sparked new ideas: Jake and Kelly Settle, Diane Wanserski, Emily Brengarth, Linda Wiederhold, Zoe Hughley, Carmen Kindling, Elissa O'Brien and Linor Vaknin.

Lastly, I would like to thank my family. They provided the foundation upon which I've had the opportunity to grow. Thanks to both sets of grandparents for introducing me to foods from all over the world, making sure that my plate was never empty and making sure that I always finished every last bite; Thanks to my parents, for keeping that tradition alive in my own house and supporting me along my journey; and lastly, to Mashette and Judy for loving me with a ferocity that makes me proud to call them my sisters.

ABOUT THE AUTHORS

DIMITRI SYRKIN-NIKOLAU is the owner of Dimo's Pizza, which has two locations in Chicago: Wrigleyville and Wicker Park. Dimo's pies are known for their outlandish ingredients and addictive tastes. They have been enjoyed by CM Punk, Andy Dick, hordes of Cubs fans, the entire improv scene in Chicago and many a folk just a few drinks in. Dimitri hopes to change the world for the better using the most delicious weapon he knows: pizza—the food of the people. He lives in Chicago, Illinois.

ANN WANSERSKI is the brand manager for Dimo's Pizza and has been with the company since February of 2009. Since her start as a general employee, she has played various roles for the company, giving her a keen eye for the offbeat flavors and quirky voice that embody all things Dimo's. She lives, bikes and eats her way

INDEX